Published by MQ Publications, Ltd.
254-258 Goswell Road, London EC1V 7EB
Copyright © MQ Publications, Ltd. 1999
All illustrations © Susie Lacome 1999

Series Editor: Ljiljana Ortolja-Baird
Editor: Jane Warren
Designer: Bet Ayer

A CIP catalogue record for this book is available
from the British Library
ISBN: Hardback 1 84072 069 7

GREAT STUFF

100 FUN PROJECTS FOR KIDS

SUSIE LACOME

MQP

contents

RAINY DAY

MAKE-BELIEVE

Most of the projects in GREAT STUFF can be made from things that can be found around the house, such as cardboard boxes, paper, fabric, Scotch tape, glue, scissors and paints. Some projects use things found in nature, like leaves, twigs, sand, shells and pebbles. A few things for some projects will need to be bought, usually from a card shop, craft shop or hardware store.

GLUE

In GREAT STUFF, unless it says so, glue always means PVA glue. PVA is excellent for sticking paper, card and cardboard and, although it goes on white, it dries clear.

Sometimes you will need to use waterproof glue – in which case use waterproof PVA – or fabric glue.

PAINT

In the same way, in this book, paint is always poster paint, unless acrylic or fabric paint is specifically listed. Poster paint is useful for painting card and paper, and is easily washed out of brushes when you are finished!

Acrylic paint sticks well to plastic surfaces, and it resists water. If you have no acrylic paint, a mixture of PVA glue and poster paint will often work just as well. In general, if you are going to paint a plastic or shiny surface, it is a good idea to sand it lightly before you begin, to give the paint a slightly rough surface to stick to.

Don't be put off if you can't find the exact color of paint or paper or size of box mentioned - most of the projects can be adapted to whatever materials you have available, and the list of materials for each project should be seen as merely a guide. Improvize, make a plan, have a go – you will probably be thrilled with the results!

THINGS TO SAVE

Cardboard boxes - all sizes

Thin card - plain + colored

Cardboard tubes - toilet paper, fax paper,
    paper towel

Paper - plain, colored, crepe, wrapping, tissue

Newspaper

Lids + tops - all sizes

Yogurt pots

Egg cartons

Matchboxes

Plastic bottles - all sizes

Styrofoam or frozen pizza backing

Plastic milk containers

Glass jars

String, raffia, ribbon,
    yarn scraps

Foam scraps

Fabric scraps

Hessian scraps

Empty cotton reels

Old socks, pantyhose, clothes

Corks

Buttons + beads

Old rubber gloves

Plastic bags

Popsicle sticks

THINGS TO FIND IN THE HOUSE

Pencil - with eraser tip

Ruler or tape measure

Color markers - with ventilated caps
    for safety

Poster paints + paintbrushes

Scissors

Pinking scissors

Tape - Scotch, parcel, masking, insulation

Glue - PVA, fabric, waterproof, glue sticks

Craft knife

Bradawl

Aluminum foil

Pasta shapes

Dried lentils + beans

Plastic wrap

Cotton

Plant canes

Plant ties

Needles - knitting, yarn, sewing

Thread

Embroidery floss pins

Safety pins

Clothes pins

String, twine

Sandpaper

NATURAL THINGS TO COLLECT

Shells

Pebbles

Glass pieces worn smooth by weathering

Autumn leaves

Twigs, sticks - no sharp points

Straw

THINGS TO BUY

Acrylic or fabric paints

Raffia - different colors

Stickers - all types

Reinforcement rings

Gold foil or card

Fusible web

Double-sided tape

Tracing paper

Marker pens - silver, gold, waterproof

Paper clips - colored

Chenille stems - colored

Paper fasteners

Wire + garden wire

Magnets

Plastic cups

Plastic drinking straws

Balloons

Plant seeds, seedlings

THINGS YOU WILL NEED

7

OUTDOOR garden

Painted Window Boxes

Cress Eggheads

Miniature Garden

Topiary Shapes

Scarecrow

Flower Wheels

Sunflower Sticks

PAINTED WINDOW BOXES

you will need...

For the Bird Window Box

Plastic window box

Sandpaper

Acrylic paints

Paintbrushes

Masking tape

Thin card, a small
   sheet

Pencil, with eraser tip

Sponge

Scissors

Allow the paint to dry before carefully lifting and repositioning the stencil (see page 25l for hints).

Use bold, contrasting colors for the best results.

Paint the window boxes only on the outside.

These butterflies are done in 2 steps: first the wings and then the body, in a contrasting color (see page 25l).

making a window box...

Bird

1 Lightly sand the window box so that the paint will stick to it. Mark a top and bottom border with masking tape. Paint the borders blue, and the center yellow.

2 Cut a bird stencil from card (see page 251)–trace one of the birds above. Stencil a row of birds on each side of the box, following Steps 3–5 on page 251).

3 Draw a zigzag pattern in pencil on the top and bottom borders. Paint over the pencil line in a contrasting color.

4 Dip the eraser tip of the pencil in paint and print dots on the birds and along the zigzag borders.

GARDEN

11

CRESS EGGHEADS

you will need...

Clean egg shells, tops taken off

Fabric, yarn + colored paper scraps

Cardboard tube, from toilet paper

Popsicle sticks, one for each egg

Cotton balls

Cress or grass seeds

Sequins, stickers,
   buttons

Paints

Paintbrushes

Color markers

Scissors

Glue

Stick on round stickers for eyes, and a pair of gold reinforcement rings for earrings.

Make a mustache and eyebrows from short fringes of yarn, and glue on a fabric tie over a paper shirt.

Wait for leaves to appear before you snip the cress for a sandwich!

This cress pup has balloon ears and a yarn tail.

making the cress eggheads...

1   Cut a popsicle stick in half and glue the 2 pieces to the bottom of a tube. Balance an egg shell on the top of the tube.

2   Paint or draw a face on the egg. Use stickers, buttons and fabric to decorate the tube body. Paint the feet.

GARDEN

3   Carefully fill the egg shell with cotton. Sprinkle with water and then with cress seeds. Put the egghead in a dark place.

4   When the green shoots appear, move the egghead to a bright place. Sprinkle water on the cotton every day.

13

MINIATURE GARDEN

you will need...

Wooden fruit crate

Popsicle sticks, cut
   in half

2 beads, 2 buttons

Paints + paintbrushes

Colour markers

Dried split peas or
   lentils, or both

Aluminum foil

Assorted colored
   paper

Wooden skewer,
   cut in half

Fabric, yarn + string
   scraps

Matchbox drawer

Matchsticks

Cotton reel, cork

Paper clip

Cocktail paper
   umbrella

Scissors

Glue

Glue paper flowers to
the walls of the crate, and
glue green fabric to a corner
post to make a tree.

Add details –
to the flowers, cat,
grass, table and
wheelbarrow – with
marker pen.

Glue a combination of
dried split peas and lentils
to the path to create
different textures.

Glue the butterflies
to the fence or the walls
of the crate.

making a miniature garden...

1 Glue popsicle sticks – rounded end up – around the crate to make a fence and gates. Glue bead handles on the gates.

2 On the *base* of the crate, draw a path and paint glue on it. Pour split peas onto the path to cover it. Shake off the extra split peas.

3 Paint the rest of the base green for grass. Glue on a pond cut from foil, and glue on yellow paper fish to swim in it.

4 Glue a bead to one end of each piece of skewer. Glue the skewers to opposite corners of the crate. Glue tiny fabric clothes (copy the ones on page 14) to yarn. Tie the yarn to the skewers.

5 For the wheelbarrow, glue button wheels on a matchbox and add matchstick handles. For the table, glue a fabric tablecloth onto the reel, and push the umbrella through a tiny hole in the middle.

6 The cat is a painted cork with *glued-on* matchstick legs, paper ears and a yarn tail. For the butterfly, fix a paper clip body to wings cut from *blue* paper (copy the ones above).

GARDEN

15

TOPIARY SHAPES

you will need...

For the Dinosaur Topiary

Wire or heavy duty garden
   wire, about 1 m (1 yd)
Fine wire scraps
Fuse wire, or other
   strong extra-fine wire
Plant pot
Paper
Pencil
Wire cutters
A few pieces of broken
   clay pot
Potting soil
2 small climbing
   plants
Plant ties
Assorted beads
Scissors

As the climbers grow, train them to the dinosaur shape using plant ties.

A wire flower with a zigzag stem makes a good topiary shape.

This simple topiary shape is the perfect way to display a flowering climber.

Heavy duty garden wire is strong, yet easy to shape without pliers – and it won't rust.

making a topiary shape...

Dinosaur

1 Draw the rough shape of a dinosaur on paper. It should be about 40 cm (16 in) long, and about 30 cm (12 in) high.

2 Bend one piece of wire to the dinosaur shape, using the wire cutters. Leave about 25 cm (10 in) extra wire at each end. Bend another piece for the inside of the legs.

3 Bend wire in a zigzag and attach it with fuse wire to the back of the dinosaur. Hang a coil of fine wire from the top of the head with fuse wire, to form an eye.

4 Put the dinosaur wire in the pot. Push the extra wire through the holes in the base, bend to lie flat under the pot and cut off the excess. Repeat for the inner leg wire.

5 Put pieces of broken clay in the pot, and fill with soil. Plant the climbers, one at each leg. Fix the climbing shoots to the wire with plant ties.

6 Loop fine wire round the pot and twist the ends together. Thread beads onto spirals made by coiling the wire round a pencil. Hook 2 or more spirals on the wire.

GARDEN

17

SCARECROW

you will need...

Garden canes, one long 2 m (2 yd) +
3 shorter 1 m (1 yd)

Twine

Pair of old rubber gloves

Large plastic plant pot

Old pair of trousers, a shirt with
 buttons + a stretchy top

2 buttons

Acrylic paints

Paintbrushes

Colored plastic
 shopping bags,
 cut into strips

Sewing thread

Needle

Straw

Scissors

Waterproof glue

Use old clothes in a large
child or adult size if you can - they
will pull on more easily over the
frame and the gloves.

Don't stuff the
scarecrow too full - just
enough to fill out the
clothes and gloves
a little.

Push the cane into
the soil of the vegetable
patch, and listen to the wind
fluttering in the flags and the
scarecrow's hair!

GREAT STUFF

18

making a scarecrow...

1 Bind a short cane across the long (body) cane for arms, using twine. Bind two canes on lower down, for legs. Stuff the gloves with straw and tie with twine to the arms. Upend the pot on the neck, for a head. Push cane through draining hole.

2 Pull on the shirt and pants, making the long cane go through a hole cut between the legs. Tie the ankles with twine. Stuff the shirt body and pants with straw. Tie the waist with twine. Remove the pot. Pull on the stretchy top. Tie the wrists with twine.

3 Upend the pot and glue on button eyes. Paint a nose, mouth and cheeks with acrylic paint. Glue on strips of plastic for hair, and a zigzag strip of plastic for a beard.

4 Replace the pot on the cane. Cut lots of small flags and streamers from plastic strips. Glue or sew them on all over the arms, legs and body of the scarecrow.

FLOWER WHEELS

you will need...

For the lobelia wheel, use a mixture of purple lobelia and bright yellow/orange marigolds for the outer ring and pink lobelia for central initial 'F'.

For the Strawberry Wheel

A level patch of soil, clear of
    weeds + stones

Garden cane (no sharp points)

Small stick

Twine, about 50 cm (20 in)

Sunflower seedling, or seed

Lettuce seeds

Chive seeds

Straw, a small bag

10-12 strawberry plant seedlings

Alpine strawberries are tiny and sweet, but any small variety will do.

The straw stops the strawberries getting too wet.

making a flower wheel...

Strawberry wheel

 1 Push the cane into the soil in the center of the patch. Tie twine to it and to a small stick, about 25 cm (10 in) away. Mark a circle in the soil, keeping the twine taut.

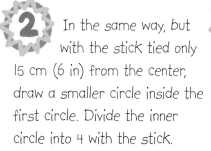 **2** In the same way, but with the stick tied only 15 cm (6 in) from the center, draw a smaller circle inside the first circle. Divide the inner circle into 4 with the stick.

 3 Plant a sunflower seed or seedling in the center of the wheel, next to the cane. You will need to tie the sunflower to the cane as it grows taller.

 4 Scatter lettuce seeds in 2 opposite quarters of the wheel, and chive seeds in the remaining quarters. Cover with a thin layer of soil and gently water the bed.

 5 Plant the strawberry seedlings in the soil of the outer ring. (They should be evenly spaced.) Gently spread straw around and between the strawberry plants.

6 Keep the flower wheel moist and free of weeds. Snip off chives as you need them, and scatter more seeds to replace the lettuces you have picked.

GARDEN

21

SUNFLOWER STICKS

Use different colors and thicknesses of twine and string for different textures.

Glue or tie one or 2 leaves and perhaps a snail to each sunflower stem, or tie/glue a colorful snail to its own cane!

Paint natural string or twine with acrylic paint to achieve the colors you want.

you will need...

Styrofoam, or
   frozen pizza backing
Assorted twine + string
Acrylic paints
Paintbrushes
Varnish
Insulation tape

Double-sided tape
Garden canes
   (no sharp points)
Assorted beads
Plant ties
Scissors
Waterproof glue

Use these bright flowers and snails in winter when the garden is looking a bit dull. Alternatively, they can be used as plant supports.

making a sunflower stick...

① Stick double-sided tape on a 6 cm (2⅜ in) square of styrofoam. Make a coil of twine or string on the sticky square. Cut the styrofoam around the coil.

② For the sunflower, cut 2 flower shapes from styrofoam. Paint them red or yellow. Glue a string coil to the center of each flower. Varnish the flower all over.

③ Tape or glue a cane to the back of one flower. Glue the other flower to the cane. (Don't try to stick the flowers together, and make sure the coils face outwards.)

④ Stick double-sided tape to a leaf cut from styrofoam (trace one above). Wind green twine round it, covering both sides. Varnish. Glue or tie to the cane.

⑤ For the snail, stick a folded string body and a coiled string shell to a styrofoam base (trace this one). Varnish. Glue beads to the feelers. Tie to the cane.

⑥ Tie a leggy plant to a sunflower stick for support, or simply pot your flower stick and enjoy year-round color. Fix the snail to a cane or glue on a pot as decoration.

OUTDOOR
wind wizardry

Pinwheels

Miniature Kites

Papier Mâché Mobiles

Wind Chimes

Airplanes

Dragon Birdscarer

Crocodile Whirligig

PINWHEELS
you will need...

For the Yellow Spotted Pinwheel

Yellow paper, about 10-18 cm
  (4-7 in) square
Green paper, a scrap
Ruler
Color markers
Stickers
Pin
Small bead
Plastic drinking straw
Piece of cork
Scissors

For an interesting pinwheel, decorate the front of the paper square differently from the back.

This pinwheel has a flower center, flowers on each of the curled corners, and a spotty design on the front.

Don't force the pinwheel tightly up against the bead, straw and cork - keep it slightly loose so that it spins more easily.

making a pinwheel...

Yellow Spot

1 Decorate both sides of the paper with color markers and stickers. With a ruler, draw 2 diagonal lines joining the opposite corners of the square.

2 Cut along the lines, but stop about 1 cm (1/4 in) from the center. You now have 4 triangles, joined in the center. Fold every alternate point into the center.

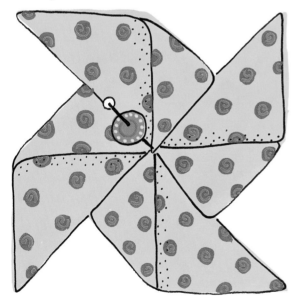

3 Cut a small circle, about 1.5 cm (1/2 in) in diameter, from green paper. Push a pin through the middle of the circle, then through alternate corners of the 4 triangles.

4 At the back, push the pin through first the bead, then the end of the straw. Bury the point in the cork, but keep the pinwheel, bead and straw slightly loose on the pin.

27

MINIATURE KITES

you will need...

Thick colored paper, about 30 cm (12 in) square

Colored paper, a large sheet

Paints

Paintbrushes

Stickers

Cord or thick thread, about 10 m (10 yd)

3 square stickers,
 or pieces of
  Scotch tape

Hole punch

Scissors

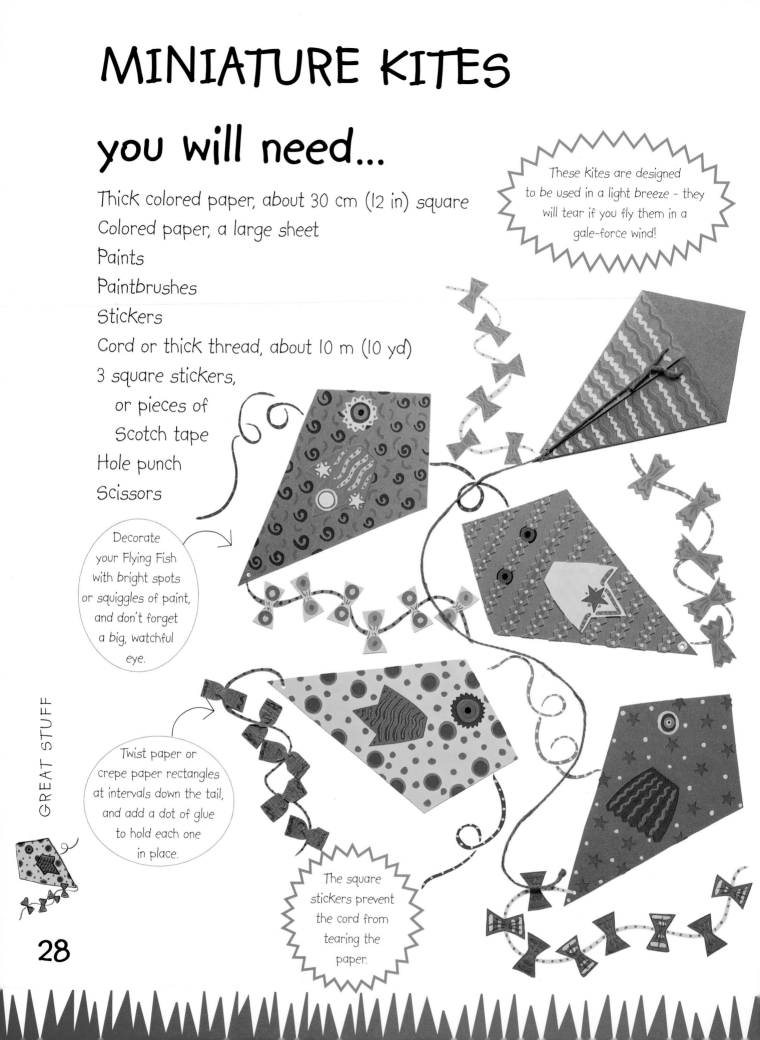

These kites are designed to be used in a light breeze - they will tear if you fly them in a gale-force wind!

Decorate your Flying Fish with bright spots or squiggles of paint, and don't forget a big, watchful eye.

Twist paper or crepe paper rectangles at intervals down the tail, and add a dot of glue to hold each one in place.

The square stickers prevent the cord from tearing the paper.

making a miniature kite...

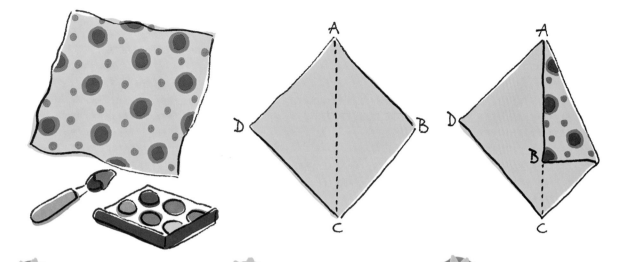

1 Decorate the square of thick paper with paint or color marker on both sides.

2 Fold the square in half along one diagonal (AC). Open the square out again.

3 Copy the picture above to fold the side AB to meet the center fold. Fold AD to meet the center fold in the same way. Flatten the folds.

4 Stick a square sticker on the tip of the kite, punch a hole and tie 1 m (1 yd) of cord through it. Twist 3 x 6 cm (1¼ x 2½ in) paper rectangles onto the tail.

5 Stick square stickers on the corners folded in at the back. Punch a hole in each. Loop cord through the holes and knot it, leaving the rest of the cord dangling.

6 Turn the kite over. On the front, paint a large eye and a fin in a contrasting color. Fly the flying fish kite by the long piece of cord tied at the back.

WIND WIZARDRY

29

PAPIER MÂCHÉ MOBILES

you will need...

For the Birds Mobile

Corrugated cardboard,
about 20 x 25 cm (8 x 10 in)

Craft Knife (be careful!)

Newspaper, cut into strips

Paints

Paintbrushes

Color markers

Stickers

Patterned wrapping paper

Paper, cut into tall
triangles (isosceles)

Varnish

Thin Knitting needle

Cord, about 75 cm (30 in)

Yarn needle

Glue, diluted with water

Glue

You can make the mobile as long as you like – just make enough birds and beads to fit your cord.

The sun, moon and stars are made from papier mâché covered in shiny foil and decorated with sequins or drawn patterns.

Draw patterns on the foil with a dry ballpoint pen to create this embossed look.

Paint the birds on both sides, or glue on patterned wrapping paper for added decoration.

making a papier mâché mobile...

Birds mobile

1 Cut 5 or 6 bird shapes from corrugated card (trace the ones on page 30) with a craft Knife. An adult should help you. The ridges should run from top to bottom.

2 Paste a layer of news-paper strips onto the birds, using dilute glue and a paintbrush (see page 245). Cover both sides and the cut edges. Allow to dry.

3 Paint the birds, or glue patterned paper on both sides. Decorate with stickers or glued-on paper and add beak, eye and wing details with color markers. Varnish.

4 Make beads by rolling the paper triangles around the Knitting needle. Glue the point of each triangle. When dry, slide off the needle. Paint and varnish the beads.

5 Gently push the Knitting needle through the middle of each bird, from top to bottom - find the gap between 2 ridges in the corrugated cardboard.

6 Tie a loop in the end of the cord. Then use the yarn needle to thread birds and beads alternately on the cord. Make a Knot below each bird/bead to stop it slipping.

WIND WIZARDRY

31

WIND CHIMES

You can make the chimes without using a drill - many of the shells you find on the beach have holes in them, and those that don't can always be tied on.

Make the rows different lengths and hang some objects from longer pieces of driftwood to give the chimes extra layers.

The glass, shells, and china knock together in the breeze and produce a tinkling sound.

you will need...

Shells, feathers, cork + bits of driftwood

Driftwood, one long piece, or garden cane

Fragments of weathered china and glass (no sharp pieces)

Twine, rope + string

Yarn needle

making the wind chimes...

1 Tie a 50 cm (20 in) length of rope or string to the middle of the long piece of driftwood. Make a loop at the other end to hang the chimes from.

2 Arrange the shells, cork, wood, glass and china into rows of different lengths. Put light things like feathers and tiny shells at the bottom. Cut the cork and wood into small pieces.

3 Ask an adult to drill holes in the shells and wood. Make holes in the cork with a needle. Thread objects onto the twine using a yarn needle, or simply loop and tie the twine round each one.

4 Tie the rows of objects loosely to the big piece of driftwood. Try to balance the weight evenly. Hang the chimes and adjust the dangling rows left and right until the wood hangs level and the objects knock against each other.

AIRPLANES

you will need...

Styrofoam, or frozen
   pizza backing
Craft Knife (be careful!)
Paints
Paintbrushes
Color markers
Stickers
Sticky putty

Cut the plane pieces from thin card if you can't find any styrofoam.

Decorate your plane with color markers, paint and stickers to look like a passenger plane or a single-seater.

Adjust the size and position of the lump of putty on the nose of plane to make it fly better.

making an airplane...

1 Cut the 3 pieces of the plane from styrofoam, using the template on page 253. (An adult should help you.)

2 Cut a notch in the body, wing and tail sections and a slit in the body of the plane. Use the picture above as a guide.

3 Paint one side of each piece. Allow to dry before painting the other side. Decorate with stickers for windows, and wing and tail markings.

4 Push the wing section through the slit in the body and slot in place. Slot the tail in place at the back of the body. Press a small lump of putty on the nose.

WIND WIZARDRY

DRAGON BIRDSCARER

you will need...

5 garden canes (no sharp points)

Raffia in several bright colors

2 orange plastic bags, fronts + backs separated

Large sheet of flexible plastic (available from hardware stores and large garden centers)

Waterproof color markers or acrylic paint

Insulation tape

Scissors

Glue
Milk carton

Push the canes into the soil where birds (or cats) are a problem – and let the wind do the rest!

Use extra canes and plastic bags of any color to make a longer tail.

Make the Dragon's face as garish – and fierce – as you can.

making a dragon birdscarer...

 1 Draw a dragon's face on the plastic sheet. Cut out. Paint the face with acrylic paint or waterproof color markers.

 2 Cut a slit for a mouth. Cut a tongue from the carton and paint it red. Poke it through the slit and tape it in place at the back.

3 Glue multicolored bunches of raffia to the back of the dragon's face for the hair, and over the slit for the tongue for a beard.

4 Tape a cane to each side of the face, at the back. Hide the top of each cane behind the raffia hair.

5 Tape the plastic sheets together to make a long tail. Cut a V-shaped notch in the last sheet.

6 Tape a cane at the join between each pair of plastic sheets. Cut lots of pennants from plastic bags. Tape pennants to the tops of the canes and the tail.

CROCODILE WHIRLIGIG

you will need...

3 plastic milk containers
Thin garden cane
6 beads, big
    enough to
    thread onto
    the cane
Green + blue acrylic
    paints
Paintbrushes
Waterproof color markers
Varnish
Insulation tape
Plastic drinking
    straw, cut
    into 3 cm
    (1¼ in) lengths
Craft knife (be careful!)
Scissors
Glue

If your beads
are too big or too
small, wrap insulation
tape around the cane
above and below each
crocodile instead.

Fold back on
a vertical side of
each triangle for
the best wind-
catching fins.

Paint each crocodile a
different color, and pick
out the details in a
contrasting color.

making a crocodile whirligig...

1 Draw a crocodile shape on the plastic container. Cut out 3 the same.

2 Mark 4 triangles on each crocodile, 2 at the front and 2 at the back. Cut 2 sides of each with the knife (an adult should help you). Fold back on the 3rd side.

3 Paint both sides of the crocodiles. On one side only, paint fins, a mouth, toes and eyes in a contrasting color. Varnish.

4 Tape a piece of straw to the back of each crocodile, in the middle.

5 Thread the crocodiles onto the cane with a bead above and below each one. A dot of glue below each bead will stop it slipping.

6 Push the cane into the ground. The wind will catch the fins and spin the crocodiles on the cane.

WIND WIZARDRY

39

OUTDOOR
waterplay

Cork Rafts +
Ducks

'Gone Fishing'
Game

Water Xylophone

Miniature
Harbor

41

CORK RAFTS + DUCKS

you will need...

For the Rafts

4 corks

Colored paper, small sheets

Stickers

2 plastic drinking straws

Craft Knife (be careful!)

Scissors

Waterproof glue

Decorate the sails in bold colors, and add paper flags.

The masts can be glued to any of the corks.

These ducks have painted paper bodies threaded onto cocktail sticks for support.

making a cork raft...

1 Glue the corks side by side to form the raft. Press them together firmly until the glue is completely dry.

2 Cut 2 square sails from paper about the length of a cork, and decorate them with stickers. Cut 2 flags from paper and add stickers for decoration.

3 Cut a slit at the top and bottom of each sail, in the center. Thread a straw through each slit. Glue a flag to the top of each straw mast.

4 Cut a small slit in the middle of 2 corks. Cut the straws to the right length. Flatten the cut ends and push each into a slit. Glue the straw masts in place.

'GONE FISHING' GAME

you will need...

Plastic milk containers, or other white
  plastic containers
Acrylic paints
Paintbrushes
Waterproof color markers
5 corks
Craft knife (be careful!)
Fine wire scraps
Sticky putty
Garden cane (no sharp points)
String, about 1 m (1 yd)
Bowl, filled with water
Scissors

Use enough putty to keep the creatures vertical in the water.

The corks will keep the creatures from sinking and escaping your hook!

Paint the creatures in bright colors which will show up even when they are under water.

Make the loops at least 1.5 cm (½ in) in diameter, otherwise you will find it very difficult to catch anything!

making the fishing game...

1 Draw a crab, starfish, octopus and 2 fish on the white plastic. Cut them out with scissors.

2 Decorate the sea creatures on both sides with acrylic paint or waterproof color markers. Make them as bright and colorful as you can.

3 Cut a slit along the length of each cork with a craft knife. (An adult should help you with this.) Slide a creature onto each cork.

4 Make a loop from a scrap of wire. Twist the ends together. Push the sharp ends into the top of a cork. Repeat for all the creatures.

5 Press one or 2 small lumps of putty onto the bottom of each creature to make sure it hangs vertically in the water.

6 Make a hook from a scrap of wire, tie it to the string and tie the end of the string to the cane. Float the creatures in water.

WATERPLAY

45

WATER XYLOPHONE

you will need...

6 glass bottles of similar size
Assorted shells + beads
Raffia + string scraps
Fine wire scraps
Blue + green ink or
    food coloring
Metal spoon
Jug
Scissors
Glue

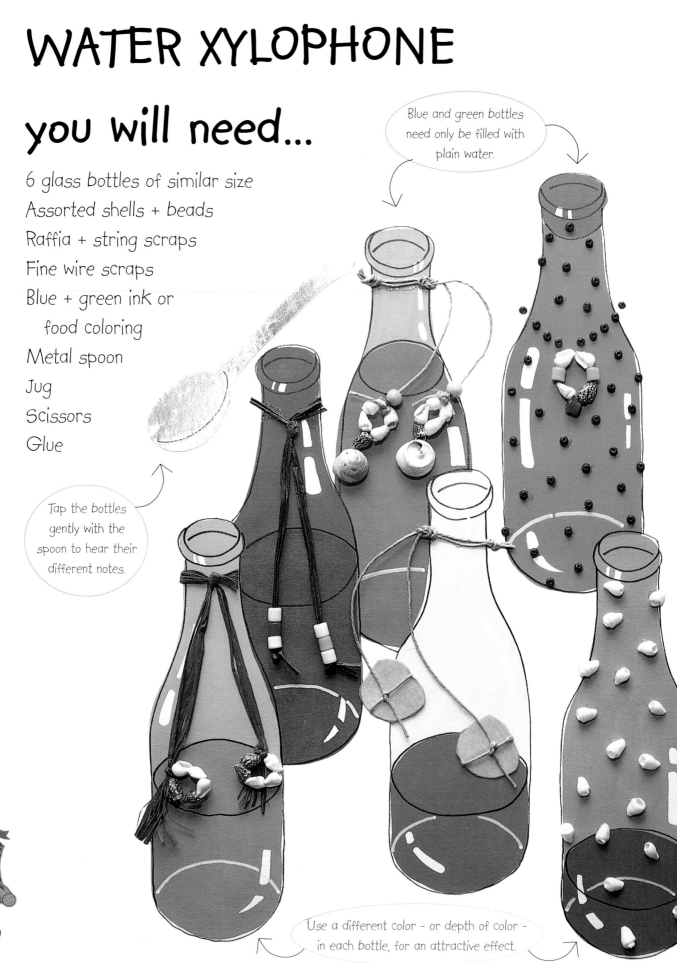

Blue and green bottles
need only be filled with
plain water.

Tap the bottles
gently with the
spoon to hear their
different notes.

Use a different color - or depth of color -
in each bottle, for an attractive effect.

GREAT STUFF

46

making a water xylophone...

1 Glue beads or shells onto the bottles,
or thread beads and shells on string or
raffia and hang round the necks of the bottles.

2 For shell tassels, thread shells on wire,
twist the wire round the ends of the
raffia and tie the raffia round the bottle neck.

3 Add ink or food coloring to a jug of
water. Use more or less ink/food
coloring to get different depths of color.

4 Line up the bottles. Pour a little water in
the first bottle, more in the next, and so
on. The last bottle should be nearly full.

WATERPLAY

47

MINIATURE HARBOR

you will need...

Large blue or green plastic bowl

Acrylic paints + paintbrushes

Waterproof color markers

Plastic bottle

2 plastic margarine tubs, with lids

Small yogurt pot

Styrofoam, or frozen pizza backing

Thin card, a small sheet

Orange + gray paper, a small sheet

Aluminum foil, a scrap

Black embroidery floss

Small pebbles or sand

2 red lids

2 corks

Matchsticks

Stickers

Red bead

Old white marker pen lids

Craft Knife

Scissors

Glue

48

The paper details on the penguins and lighthouse will be spoiled if you get them wet - take care!

You may find it easier to glue the matchsticks and thread into a Kind ladder, and then glue the completed railing to the lighthouse.

Don't fill the bowl with water, put in just enough to let your whale and ship float freely.

You can use any plastic food container for the base of the lighthouse and the ship; take-out cartons are a good choice.

When you have made the lighthouse, boat and whales, position them in a large bowl and partially fill with water.

making a miniature harbor...

1 Paint red and white stripes on the bottle and a black strip around the top. Use stickers for a door and windows. Don't paint or decorate the bottom 6 cm (2³⁄₈ in) of the bottle.

2 Paint the small pot yellow. Add hatching with color marker. Upend and glue to the top of the bottle. Glue a bead on top. Glue on matchsticks round the black stripe and a black thread rail.

3 Draw round the bottle base on one tub lid. Cut out the circle. Paint the tub and lid brown. Put pebbles in the base, replace the lid and push the bottle through it. Put the lighthouse in the bowl.

4 Cut holes for the 2 funnels in the tub lid. Paint the tub and lid white and add port holes on both sides. Glue styrofoam smoke (copy the smoke above) to the lids. Push the lids through the holes.

5 Cut 2 whales from card. Cover with foil. Cut a slit along the length of each cork with the craft knife (an adult should help you). Slide a whale onto each cork.

6 Paint old pen lids black, leaving an oval white. Paint on eyes and a beak. Cut feet from orange paper and wings from gray paper (copy the ones above) and glue to the penguins.

WATERPLAY

49

OUTDOOR
games to play

Penguin Skittles

Throw the Dog
a Bone

Knock the Parrots
off their Perch

Cup-and-Ball
Game

Jump Rope

PENGUIN SKITTLES

you will need...

10 plastic bottles and lids, all the same size

Plastic bag or old rubber gloves

Acrylic paints

Paintbrushes

Color markers

Jug

Sand (optional)

Small ball

The sand or water helps keep the bottles steady until you are ready to bowl them over!

Draw a pupil on each eye and make the penguins look in different directions, just for fun.

Paint the lids for added color if you like.

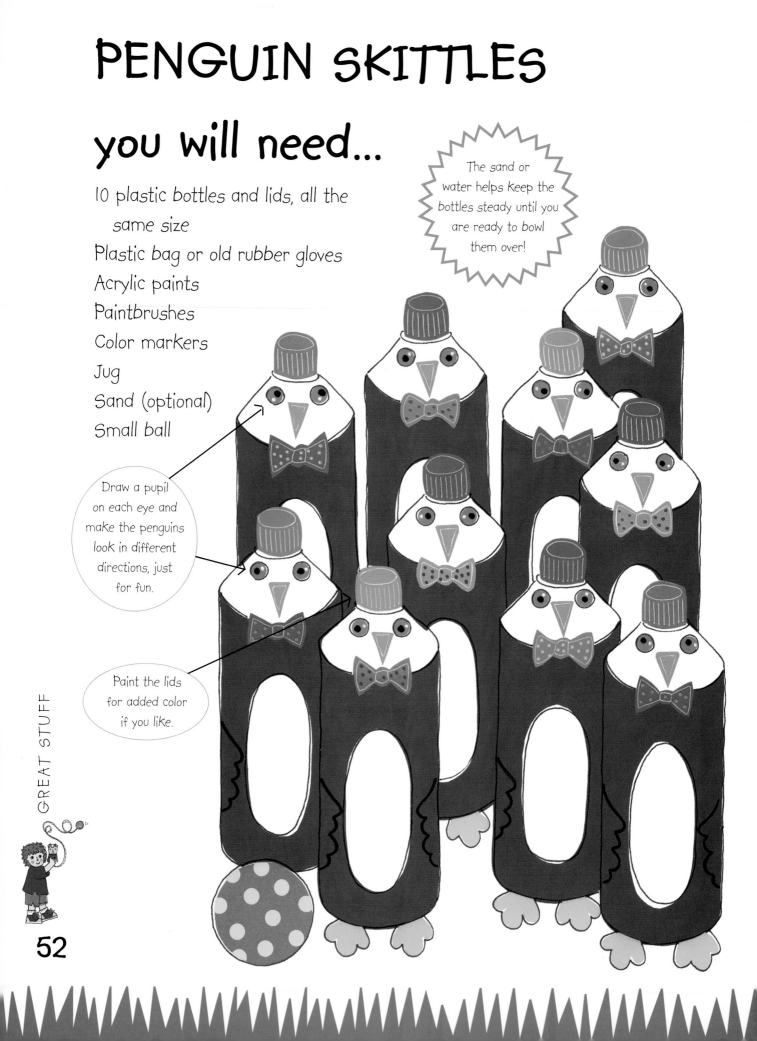

making the penguin skittles...

1 Paint a white oval tummy on each bottle. Paint the neck of each bottle white. Allow to dry.

2 Paint the rest of each bottle black. Take care not to spoil the white areas. Allow to dry.

3 Paint (or draw in color marker) a red bow tie, an orange beak, blue/green eyes and black pupils.

4 Cut up the plastic bag to make 2 feet for each penguin. Glue them to the base of the bottle. Draw on wings with color marker.

5 Quarter fill each bottle with sand (or water), using a jug. Try not to wet the paint. Replace the lids and tighten.

6 Set the skittles up in a group. Bowl the ball towards them and see how many penguins you can knock over in one go!

GAMES TO PLAY

53

THROW THE DOG A BONE

Make sure your beanbags will fit through the mouth you have cut.

Prop the cardboard against a wall, or against a pair of small plant pots.

You could throw the dog a tennis ball instead of the beanbags.

Make small square beanbags as a simpler alternative.

you will need...

Thick cardboard, about 24 cm (9½ in) square

Pencil

Craft knife (be careful!)

Paints + paintbrushes

Dried beans

Hessian or fabric, about 16 cm (6½ in) square

Sewing thread

Needle

Scissors + pinking scissors

Glue

making a dog and bones...

 1 On the cardboard, draw a border and a dog with a mouth about 7.5 cm (3 in) in diameter. Cut out the mouth with a craft knife (an adult should help you).

2 Paint the dog, the background and the border in bright contrasting colors. Copy the picture above or choose your own color combinations.

 3 Cut out 2 ears from hessian. Glue the top third of each ear to the cardboard, leaving the bottom two-thirds to flap free.

4 For a beanbag, cut 2 bone shapes from fabric using pinking scissors. Sew them together, leaving a gap. Stuff with beans and sew up the gap.

GAMES TO PLAY

55

KNOCK THE PARROTS OFF THEIR PERCH

you will need...

6 soda cans, clean + empty
Dried beans
Scotch tape
Thin card, a small sheet
Acrylic paints
Paintbrushes
Color markers
Stickers
2 plant pots
2 long garden
    canes
Tennis ball

Use bright acrylic paint and color markers to make brilliant plumage for your parrots.

Paint or draw the eyes and add round stickers for the finishing touch.

Decorate the plant pots with acrylic paint – if you have permission!

Throw the ball and try to knock the parrots off their perch!

making the parrots + perch...

1 Cut 6 circles from card to fit the top of a can (draw round the end of a can). Pour a handful of beans into each can. Tape over the hole. Glue a circle to the top of each can.

2 Paint the cans all over in bright colors. Paint the card tops a contrasting color. Allow to dry.

3 Paint (or draw) the parrots' eyes, beaks, wings and tails. Decorate the tops with spots and stripes.

4 Rest the canes about 5 cm (2 in) apart on the upturned pots. Stand the parrots on their cane perch.

CUP-AND-BALL GAME

you will need...

For one Cup-and-Ball

2 yogurt pots, clean + empty

Paints

Paintbrushes

Color markers

Foam shapes or scraps

Stickers

Masking tape

Ribbon or braid

Colored paper scraps

Ping pong ball

Yarn or knitting needle

String or cord, about
50 cm (20 in)

Scissors

Glue

This Funny Face has pointy foam ears and a mustache made from a strip of plastic.

The Knot hidden in the top pot Keeps the string secure.

Throw the ball up and try to catch it in your Funny Face cup.

making a cup-and-ball game...

1 Paint the yogurt pots. Paint a pattern on one, or use stickers. Glue a foam nose and sticker eyes to the other.

2 Glue the bases of the pots together. Tape over the join to strengthen it. Glue ribbon, braid or colored paper over the join.

3 Knot the string onto the ball. Stick tape all over the ball. Cover the knot with tape, but leave the string dangling free. Paint the ball and add stickers for decoration.

4 Make a hole in the bases of the 2 pots with a yarn needle. Push the string through the hole in the bottom pot. Knot the end to hold it in the top pot.

GAMES TO PLAY

59

JUMP ROPE

you will need...

Colored nylon cord in 4 colors:
  3 colors each about 2 m (2 yd)
  A scrap of a fourth color
Assorted wooden beads
Scissors

This yellow beaded cord has been tied on at both ends to decorate the finished jump rope.

Remember that braiding will shorten your rope, so start off with a generous length - you can always cut it!

Make a longer jump rope if you plan to skip with your friends.

making a jump rope...

1   Knot the 3 strands of rope together at one end, leaving about 25 cm (10 in) free below the knot.

2   Hook the knot onto a coat hook or cupboard handle to hold it still. Braid the rope, keeping the tension even as you go.

3   Stop braiding about 25 cm (10 in) before the end. Knot the 3 strands of rope together.

4   Thread beads onto each strand of rope, tying knots to hold them in place. Tie a small, beaded cord just above the knots in the rope. Unravel the ends to make tassels.

GAMES TO PLAY

61

PARTY TIME
birthdays

62

Birthday Banner

Animal Balloons

Party Cups

Party Hats

Party Bags

Birthday T-shirts

63

BIRTHDAY BANNER

The triangles glued over the corners will stop the string from tearing the paper when the banner is hung up.

Use a gold marker pen, gold star stickers and gold paper to give extra sparkle to the banner.

Let your imagination run wild, and make each crown and party hat different.

You can make this party banner as long as your piece of string – just keep adding squares or rectangles!

you will need...

Assorted colored paper, large sheets
Foil or gold paper, large sheets
Raffia or yarn or tissue strips,
   cut into 15 cm (6 in) lengths
Yarn or string or raffia, about 3 m (3 yd)

Stickers
Color markers
Hole punch
Scissors
Glue

making a birthday banner...

 1 Cut out 18 cm (7 in) squares and 12 x 18 cm (5 x 7 in) rectangles from paper in lots of different colors. Cut 8 squares and 8 rectangles in total.

2 Cut 16 small 4 cm (1½ in) squares from colored paper. Cut each in half, to make 2 triangles. Glue a triangle to the top 2 corners of the squares and rectangles. Punch holes in these corners.

3 Cut 8 crown and 8 cone shapes from foil and colored paper. If you need any help, trace off the cone and crown shapes on page 70.

4 Glue a crown in the middle of each large square, and a cone in the middle of each rectangle. Make sure that the corners with triangles are at the top.

5 Glue small bunches of raffia, yarn or tissue strips onto the cone hats. Decorate the crowns and hats with stickers, color markers and glued-on paper shapes.

6 Thread a length of yarn, string or raffia through the holes in the corners, alternating squares (crowns) and rectangles (cones) as you go.

BIRTHDAYS

ANIMAL BALLOONS

you will need...

For the Orange Cat Balloon

Orange balloon

Yarn or narrow ribbon,
    about 75 cm (30 in)

Green or yellow
    round stickers

Foam scraps

Yellow plastic
    drinking straw

Orange fabric or
    paper scraps

Glue or double-sided tape

Color markers

Scissors

Two white balloons covered with color marker spots make delightful ears for the Dalmatian!

A bow round his neck makes this pooch look like a pedigree!

Miss Pig's ears and nose are cut from pieces of pink foam, and her eyes are blue stickers.

A long, green wiggly balloon makes a long, green wriggly caterpillar – just add sticker eyes and bright markings of your own design.

66

making an animal balloon...

Orange Cat

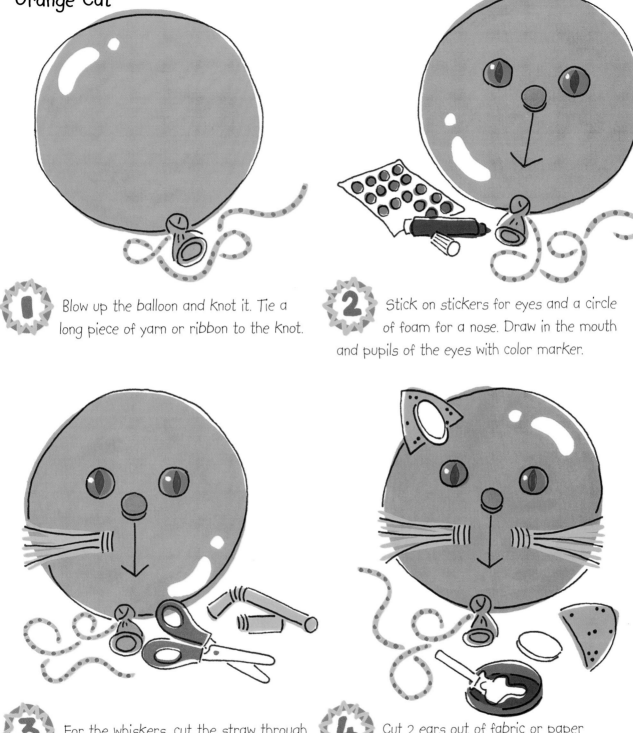

1 Blow up the balloon and knot it. Tie a long piece of yarn or ribbon to the knot.

2 Stick on stickers for eyes and a circle of foam for a nose. Draw in the mouth and pupils of the eyes with color marker.

3 For the whiskers, cut the straw through the bend, and about 7.5 cm (3 in) below it. Cut this in half along its length. In each half make 6-8 cuts up to the bend. Glue the bend of the straw to the balloon.

4 Cut 2 ears out of fabric or paper (a bulgy triangle makes a good ear shape). Glue an oval of white foam to the front of each ear. Glue the ears in place on the balloon.

67

PARTY CUPS

you will need...

For the Frog Cup

Paper cup

Plastic drinking straw

Dark green, light green, orange +
  yellow paper, small sheets

Round yellow stickers

Paints

Paintbrush

Color markers

Craft knife (be careful!)

Scissors, pinking scissors

Glue

Snail's feelers are made from small beads threaded onto paper string and glued in place.

Draw around the two ends of your cup to get the flower circles you need.

Bee's delicate wings are cut from pale blue tissue.

making a frog cup...

(1) Cut a frog body/head/front legs from dark green paper and 2 back legs from light green paper.

(2) Glue the frog's back legs to the back of the body. Stick on yellow stickers for eyes. Paint on the details, or use a color marker. Glue the frog onto the cup.

(3) From paper, cut a large flower shape. With pinking scissors, cut a smaller paper circle and glue on the front of the flower.

(4) Cut 2 slits in the center of the flower with the craft knife (an adult should help you). Thread the straw through the slits.

PARTY HATS

you will need...

For the Cone Hat

Thin colored card, about 40 cm
   (16 in) square
Assorted colored paper, small sheets
Assorted colored tissue paper,
   scraps cut into thin strips
Star stickers + round stickers
Shirring elastic, about 40 cm
   (16 in)
Yarn needle
Pencil
Pinking scissors
Scissors
Glue or double-sided
   tape or stapler

Make tiny tassels
by folding a bunch of
4 tissue strips in half,
and holding the fold
down with a bright
sticker.

Cut a zigzag down
one long edge of a strip
of gold card to make
this glittering crown.

Staple the elastic to the
inside of the hat on each
side if you prefer.

Big shiny
stickers look like
crown jewels, and a
scattering of tiny stars
- one on each point -
catch the light
and add extra
sparkle.

making a party hat...

Cone

 Cut strips of colored paper using pinking scissors. Glue the strips diagonally across the square of colored card.

 Draw around a dinner plate on the card. Cut out the circle with scissors. Cut away a quarter section (see page 246).

 Decorate the card with stickers. Make small bunches of tissue strips into tiny tassels (see page 249), and stick them down with stickers. Make sure all the tassels hang away from the center.

 Glue, tape or staple the card into a cone to fit round your head. Stick a large tassel to the top. Make a hole on each side of the hat with the needle. Thread elastic through the holes and knot on the outside.

71

PARTY BAGS

you will need...

For the Flop-eared Bunny Bag

Blue paper, about 15 x 40 cm (6 x 16 in)

Pale pink crepe paper, about 10 cm
(4 in) square

Deep pink crepe paper, 2 strips each
about 1.5 x 8 cm (½ x 3¼ in)

2 pink balloons

Raffia, 2 lengths each
about 40 cm (16 in)

6 round blue stickers

Color markers

Foam scrap

Hole punch

Pinking scissors

Scissors

Glue

This dog is the proud owner of a brown crepe paper patch – and a sloppy balloon tongue!

A strip of foam makes a soft handle.

Make bags to suit a birthday theme, or try this simple flower, perfect for any party.

Paint the foam scrap if necessary before you glue it in place.

The tractor is cut from colored paper and given a shiny candy wrapper as a rear tire.

making a party bag...

Flop-eared Bunny

1 Fold the blue paper in half. Trim the short ends with pinking scissors. Glue on an oval cut from pale pink crepe paper. Glue on balloon ears.

2 Add stickers for eyes, and glue on the foam nose. Draw in a mouth with color marker.

3 Cut the pieces of deep pink paper into very thin strips, stopping about 1.5 cm (½ in) from the end. Glue these whiskers on either side of the mouth.

4 On the inside of the bag, put a sticker where you will make the holes for the 2 handles. Punch the holes (4 in all). Thread raffia or foam handles through the holes and knot on the outside.

5 Open out the bag and lay it wrong side up. Spread glue down each of the long sides.

6 Fold the bag in half again, pressing the 2 sides together and allow the glue to set. Staple the sides for extra strength.

BIRTHDAY T-SHIRTS

you will need...

For the No. 5 T-shirt

Cotton T-shirt

Yellow fabric, about 25 cm (10 in) square

Patterned fabric, about 25 cm (10 in) square

Fusible web (see page 248)

4 buttons

Paper

Sewing thread

Needle + pins

Iron (be careful!)

Pinking scissors

Scissors

Make a birthday T-shirt to wear at your own party, or give it as a gift to a friend.

Choose fabric of your favorite color, making sure that the number fabric shows up against the background fabric.

Cut out a petal pattern from bright background material and fuse on a circle of check fabric for this sunflower T-shirt.

GREAT STUFF

74

making a birthday T-shirt...

No. 5

1 Iron fusible web to the wrong side of the yellow fabric and the patterned fabric (*see page 248*). An adult should help you with this.

2 Cut the yellow fabric to fit the T-shirt. Trim the edges of the yellow fabric with pinking scissors.

3 Make a paper pattern of the number you need to fit on the yellow background fabric. Pin it to the right side of the patterned fabric and cut out.

 Remove the paper backing from the fabric number. Carefully place the number in the center of the yellow fabric. Iron over the number to make it stick (an adult should help you).

 Remove the paper backing from the yellow fabric. Place the yellow fabric on the front of the T-shirt. Iron over it to make it stick to the T-shirt (an adult should help you).

 Sew a button to each corner of the yellow square, stitching through all the layers. Glue the buttons on if you prefer.

BIRTHDAYS

75

PARTY TIME
Easter holiday

Easter Paper Chain

'Rattle and Roll' Puzzle

Salt Dough Easter Tree

Royal Eggs

Decorated Eggs

Easter Bonnets

EASTER PAPER CHAIN

you will need...

For the Ducklings Paper Chain

White paper, strip of
   10 x 54 cm (4 x 21½ in)
Pencil + color marker
Paints + paintbrushes
Scissors

Use a longer strip of paper -
or tape 2 strips together - for a
longer paper chain.

Carefully cut away the
paper under the beak.

The Bunnies touch noses
and tails at the paper folds
and edges.

GREAT STUFF

78

making a paper chain...

Ducklings

1 Fold the paper strip concertina-style 5 times. You should have a book about 9 cm x 10 cm (3½ x 4 in).

2 Draw a duckling in pencil on the top page of the book. Make sure the tummy, beak and tail reach the edge or fold at the sides. Cut round the top of the duckling through all the layers.

3 Open out the concertina. You will have 6 duckling silhouettes. Draw in their wings, eyes and beaks to match the duckling you drew.

4 Color the ducklings and their pond with paints or color markers. Try painting alternate ducklings in different colors.

'RATTLE AND ROLL' PUZZLE

you will need...

For the Easter Egg Puzzle

Round cheese box with clear plastic lid

Styrofoam or frozen pizza backing

Paints

Paintbrushes

Color markers

5 dried peas or beans

Narrow ribbon, about 25 cm (10 in)

Scotch tape or plastic wrap

Pencil

Scissors

Shake the puzzle and try to get all the peas into the bunnies' eyes at the same time.

Have fun decorating the lid and box with paints or color markers.

If your cheese box has a cardboard lid, cut out a circle from the middle and stretch a piece of plastic wrap across the gap - now you can see inside without losing the peas!

Put the same number of peas into the box as there are holes.

making an Easter puzzle...

Easter Egg

1 Take the card disk out of the base of the box. Draw round it to make a disk from styrofoam. Draw an Easter egg and bow on the styrofoam.

2 Mark the position of 5 holes in the bow. Push the end of the pencil into the styrofoam, hard enough to make a dent at each mark. (You do not need to make an actual hole.)

3 Decorate the box, inside and out, with paint or color markers. Decorate the lid too.

4 Paint the Easter egg and bow in bright colours on the styrofoam disk. Put the card disk and then the painted disk back in the box.

5 Put 5 dried peas into the box. Put the lid on and seal it with sticky tape or plastic wrap.

6 Make a small ribbon bow. Glue it to the side of the box.

EASTER HOLIDAY

81

SALT DOUGH EASTER TREE

you will need...

Cardboard scraps

Salt dough (*see page 252*)

Twiggy branch

Plant pot

Broad ribbon, about 1 m (1 yd)

Small pebbles, enough to fill
   the plant pot

Embroidery floss
   or narrow ribbon,
   about 1 m (1 yd)

Paints

Paintbrushes

Rolling pin

Knife

Skewer

Pencil

Scissors

The number of eggs you
need will depend on the size of the branch
you have chosen, and the size of the
eggs you make.

Experiment
with different
designs and
colors.

You may need to
glue the ribbon to
the pot, to stop it
slipping down.

Pack the
pebbles all
around the
stem of the
branch, making
sure it stands
upright.

making an Easter tree...

1 Draw an egg shape on the cardboard in pencil. Cut it out.

2 Roll out the salt dough to a thickness of about 0.5 cm (1/8 in). Cut round the cardboard egg to make egg shapes from dough. Make a hole in each egg with a skewer. Bake the eggs (see page 252).

3 When the dough eggs are cool, paint them in pastel colors on both sides. Allow the paint to dry.

4 Paint on wavy lines, dots, stars and hearts in contrasting colors. Thread a piece of embroidery floss or ribbon through each hole and make a loop.

5 Paint the twiggy branch pale blue. You may need to give it more than one coat.

6 Paint the pot yellow. Tie ribbon round it and make a bow. Pack pebbles round the branch to keep it upright. Hang the eggs from the tree.

83

ROYAL EGGS

The Queen's earrings are made by threading beads and a sequin onto thread, then gluing the free end of the thread to the egg.

The shape of the crown is up to you - here are some designs you might like to copy.

Yarn or raffia, cut into short pieces, makes good hair.

Cover the head with gummed colored paper, glue on a pair of tiny yarn braids and finish with pretty ribbon bows.

you will need...

For the King

Egg, hardboiled

Cardboard tube, about 3 cm (1¼ in) long

Gold paper, a strip about 4 x 15 cm (1½ x 6 in)

Black tissue paper, narrow strips

Paints + paintbrushes

Color markers

Round stickers, sequins

Scissors

Glue or Scotch tape

making a royal egg...

King

 1 Paint the cardboard tube to look like a collar. Place the egg on it when it is dry.

2 Stick on round sticker eyes, and draw a nose and cheeks with color markers.

3 Glue tissue paper strips onto the head for hair. Glue a fringe of shorter tissue strips below the nose for a mustache.

4 Cut a crown from gold paper. Decorate it with sequins and stickers. Tape the ends together to fit round the head and glue or tape it on the egg.

85

DECORATED EGGS

To spray a fine mist of paint onto the egg, draw your finger gently across the toothbrush bristles.

Stamp dots at random, or make a formal pattern.

Paste on different colors of tissue to create an interesting, layered effect.

Paste a deep pink tissue heart onto a pale pink tissue-covered egg and give it as a gift to someone you love.

you will need...

For the Speckled Egg
Egg, hardboiled
Paints + paintbrushes
Old toothbrush
Newspapers

For the Spotted Egg
Egg, hardboiled
Paints + paintbrushes
Pencil, with eraser tip

For the Tissue Paper Egg
Egg, hardboiled
Colored tissue paper
Paintbrush
Glue, diluted with water

making the decorated eggs...

Speckled

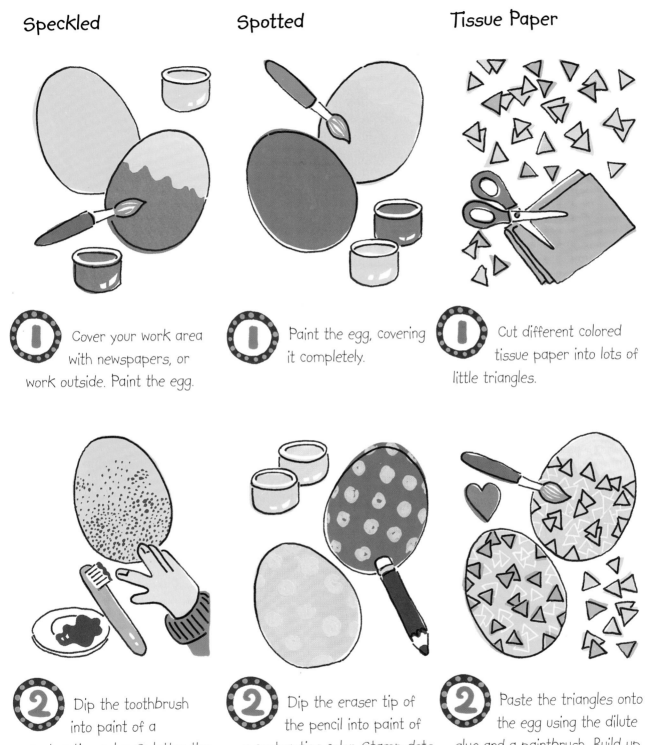

1 Cover your work area with newspapers, or work outside. Paint the egg.

2 Dip the toothbrush into paint of a contrasting color. Splatter the egg with paint by drawing your finger across the bristles.

Spotted

1 Paint the egg, covering it completely.

2 Dip the eraser tip of the pencil into paint of a contrasting color. Stamp dots of paint in a pattern or at random all over the egg.

Tissue Paper

1 Cut different colored tissue paper into lots of little triangles.

2 Paste the triangles onto the egg using the dilute glue and a paintbrush. Build up layers of tissue until the whole egg is covered.

EASTER HOLIDAY

87

EASTER BONNETS

you will need...

For the Chicks Bonnet

Cardboard scraps

Green card, about 45 cm (18 in) square

Red card, about 20 cm (8 in) square

Green crepe paper, about 20 cm (8 in) square

Ribbon, two pieces each about 35 cm (13½ in) long

A ball of yellow yarn

Round blue stickers

Black marker pen

Stapler or Scotch tape

Scissors

Glue

> Glue the feet on at different angles to make the chicks more fun.

> For the Bunnies bonnet, glue a trio of gray rabbits – trace these if you like – around the brim of a cone made from blue card.

> The whiskers, noses and inner ears are made from crepe paper.

GREAT STUFF

88

making an Easter bonnet...

Chicks

1 Make 5 yellow pompoms (see page 250 for instructions). Make 10 pompoms if you want chicks at the back of the bonnet too.

2 Make a cone from a circle of green card the size of a dinner plate (see page 246). Tape or staple the cone in shape.

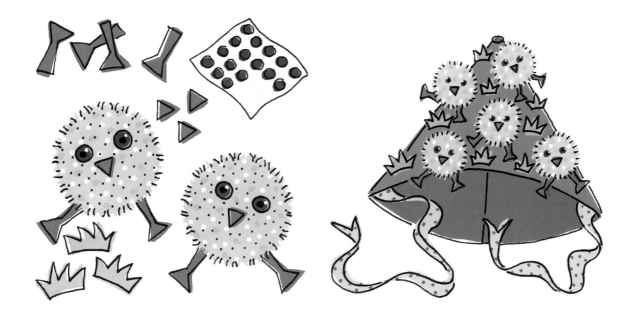

3 Cut 2 feet and 1 beak from red card for each chick (copy the ones above). Glue them on the chicks, and add stickers for eyes. Cut zigzag tufts of grass from crepe paper.

4 Glue the chicks onto the bonnet. Glue the grass in the spaces between the chicks. Staple a ribbon inside the bonnet on each side. Tie the ribbon under your chin.

89

PARTY TIME
Hallowe'en

Spooky Lanterns

Hallowe'en Mobile

Jiggly Skeleton

Trick or Treat
Party Bags

Jack-o'-lantern

Leafy Monsters

91

SPOOKY LANTERNS

you will need...

For the Cat Lantern

Glass jar

Orange + yellow tissue paper, torn
  into strips

Black paper, about 10 cm (4 in) square

String, raffia or cord, about 1 m (1 yd)

2 beads

Pencil

Paintbrush

Small candle
  or tea light

Scissors

Glue, diluted
  with water

You can use any color of tissue paper for these lanterns, but cut the silhouettes out of black paper for the spookiest results!

Capture your own midnight sky with this lantern – cover the jar with dark blue and black tissue, glue on a sleepy crescent moon, and finish with a sprinkling of sticker stars.

Cut these creepy spiders out of black paper and make them scuttle in all directions over your jar.

making a spooky lantern...

Cat

① Paste tissue strips onto the jar using dilute glue and a paintbrush. Cover the jar completely.

② Fold the black paper in half. Draw half a cat's face next to the fold (copy the picture above). Cut out eyes, nose, mouth and whiskers and cut around the head. Cut 2 pupils.

③ Glue the cat face and pupils onto the jar. Knot a bead onto each end of a 75 cm (30 in) piece of string. Tie the shorter piece of string around the top of the jar, catching in the beaded ends of the longer piece.

④ Put a small candle or tea light into the jar. Use the long, beaded string to carry the lantern, or to hang it from a branch.

HALLOWE'EN MOBILE

you will need...

Cardboard box

Newspaper, torn into strips

Red, black + orange paper,
    small sheets

Paints

Paintbrushes

Color marker

Bristles, from an old brush

Yarn or thread, 5 lengths each about
    15 cm (6 in)

Round blue + star stickers

2 small beads

2 small buttons

Yarn needle

Pencil

Scissors

Glue

Glue, diluted with water

You may prefer to sew on the Cat's button eyes and mouth.

Hang the mobile from a loop of yarn.

The Bat's inner ears and the Hat's crescent moon are cut from orange paper and glued in place.

Add details with color markers.

Make the Spider's legs extra long and creepy.

making a Hallowe'en mobile...

 1 Cut a cat, bat, pumpkin, witch's hat and spider out of cardboard (trace the ones opposite).

2 Paste newspaper strips onto the shapes using a paintbrush and dilute glue (see page 245). Allow to dry.

3 Paint all the shapes white. Allow to dry. Then paint the cat and spider black, the bat gray, the hat purple, and the pumpkin orange/green.

 4 Glue on the cat's button eyes, bristle whiskers and red paper nose and inner ears. Glue black paper cut outs on the pumpkin. Glue bristle whiskers on the bat and add sticker eyes.

 5 Stick star stickers and a paper moon on the hat. The spider's eyes are glued-on beads. For legs, fold 4 long strips of black paper concertina-style and glue the middle of each strip to the body.

6 Thread the needle with a length of yarn and link the top of the spider with the bottom of the hat. Link the hat and pumpkin with another length of yarn, and so on. Tie the top length in a loop.

95

JIGGLY SKELETON

you will need...

White card, 2 large sheets
White wax crayon or candle
Black paint or ink
Paintbrush
13 paper fasteners
Yarn or string, about 30 cm (12 in)
Yarn needle
Pencil
Scissors

Hang the skeleton from your finger and make it dance!

Give the skeleton large eye sockets and a ghoulish grin.

Draw a 'back view' of the skeleton on the back of the card body parts and make it look spooky from all directions!

If you have enough card, you could make the skeleton life-sized.

making a jiggly skeleton...

1 Draw body parts in pencil on white card (trace the skeleton opposite). You need 1 head, 1 body, 4 arm parts, 2 hands, 4 leg parts, and 2 feet. Cut out.

2 Copying the picture on page 96, draw the outline of bones, eye sockets and a mouth in pencil. Fill in the outlines with crayon.

3 Paint all the card pieces black. (The crayon will not take the paint and so the white bones of the skeleton will show through.)

4 Lay the skeleton out so that the head, arms, legs, hands and feet are in place. Punch a hole with the needle through both layers where the pieces overlap.

5 Push a paper fastener through each hole and open it out at the back.

6 Thread the needle with yarn and punch a hole at the top of the skull. Make a loop with the yarn and tie the ends so that you can hang the skeleton up.

TRICK OR TREAT PARTY BAGS

For the Witch's Hat bag, glue two pieces together and decorate with sparkly star stickers.

The Cat has black-on-yellow sticker eyes and frayed crepe paper whiskers glued on either side of a painted nose.

YOU will need...

For the Pumpkin Bag

Orange crepe paper, about 20 x 30 cm (8 x 12 in)

Green crepe paper, about 30 cm (12 in) square

Black crepe paper, about 5 x 10 cm (2 x 4 in)

Raffia, 2 lengths each about 40 cm (16 in)

4 square or round stickers, or small pieces of Scotch tape

Pencil
Hole punch
Scissors
Glue

Make sure you strengthen the holes for the handles with stickers or pieces of Scotch tape, otherwise the bag will tear as you fill it with candy.

making a party bag...

Pumpkin

 Fold the orange crepe paper in half so that it measures about 20 x 15 cm (8 x 6 in). Glue the sides closed but leave the top open.

 Cut out 2 sets of 2 leaves and a stalk from green paper (copy the picture on page 98). Glue a set of leaves to the top edge of the bag, front and back.

 From black paper, cut 3 triangles for the eyes and nose, and a row of teeth (copy the ones in the picture if you need to). Glue them on the front of the bag.

 On the inside of the bag, put a sticker where you will make holes for the handles. Punch the holes (4 in all). Thread raffia handles through the holes and knot on the outside.

HALLOWE'EN

JACK-O'-LANTERN

you will need...

For the Pumpkin Face

Pumpkin

Craft Knife (be careful!)

Spoon

Pencil

Whole cloves

Dried orange slices
  (see page 246)

Metal skewer

Yarn or twine,
  about 1.5 m (1½ yd)

Yarn needle

Tea light or
  night light or
  candle

Cut slices of orange in advance and dry them slowly in a cool oven or ner a heater.

Make sure the earrings dangle on a level with the cheeks.

For a really different lantern, let candlelight shine out through stars, moons and tiny holes cut out all round the pumpkin.

making a jack-o'-lantern...

Face

 1 Cut a zigzag around the top of the pumpkin with the craft knife (an adult should help you), and put this lid to one side. Scoop out the flesh and seeds of the pumpkin. Do not make the shell too thin.

2 Draw eyes, nose, mouth and star cheeks on the front of the pumpkin in pencil. Cut out the eyes, nose and mouth with the craft knife (an adult should help you). Press cloves into the cheeks.

3 Push 2 holes in each side of the pumpkin with a skewer. With the needle, thread each orange slice onto a 30 cm (12 in) piece of yarn. Tie each on the inside of the pumpkin, leaving the orange earring to dangle.

4 To make a handle, tie each end of a 75 cm (30 in) length of yarn to the sides of the pumpkin, using the earring holes. Put the tea light inside the pumpkin and replace the lid.

LEAFY MONSTERS

you will need...

Assorted leaves in autumn colors

Dark paper, a large sheet

Dried pulses (lentils, peas)
   or popcorn kernels

Straw

Old phone book

Some heavy books

Scissors

Glue

Use your imagination and create some weird and wonderful new creatures!

This bloated beastie has long leaf legs, straw arms, frazzled ferny hair and a large red leaf for a mouth.

A snake with legs? A lizard with hair? Make this fierce monster from a variety of brightly-colored leaves, carefully matched for size.

102

Choose a dark color for your background paper to show the monsters off at their best

making a leafy monster...

 1 Collect leaves in as many colors, shapes and sizes as you can.

2 Press the leaves immediately by placing them between the pages of the phone book. Shut the book and put some heavy books on top, to add weight. Leave them for two weeks.

3 Arrange the leaves on backing paper. Make monsters, insects and weird animals using different leaves for bodies, legs, ears, hands and feelers. Use pulses for eyes.

4 When you are happy with your creatures, glue the leaves in place on the paper.

HALLOWE'EN

PARTY TIME
Christmas fun

Candy Wreath

Christmas Stocking

Tree Fairy

Fingerprint Robin
Cards + Tags

Painted Pasta
Garland + Star

Raffia Reindeer
+ Straw Star

Potato Stamp
Gift Wrap

CANDY WREATH

you will need...

Green card, about 40 cm (16 in) square

Yellow card, a large sheet

Small sprigs of spruce, enough to fill a plastic shopping bag

Assorted colored paper, scraps

Double-sided tape

Yarn needle

Red yarn

Cup, about 9 cm (3½ in) in diameter

Cup, about 6 cm (2⅜ in) in diameter

2 sizes of dinner plate

13 wrapped sweets

Broad red ribbon, about 1 m (1 yd)

Scissors

Glue

You can look forward to eating the candy when you take down the wreath and other decorations.

Give the candy wrappers extra sparkle using a gold or silver marker pen.

An easy way to make a star is to glue together 2 paper squares so that the corners make the eight points of a star.

If you don't have spruce, any evergreen will do; or you can glue on leaves cut from green crepe paper.

making a candy wreath...

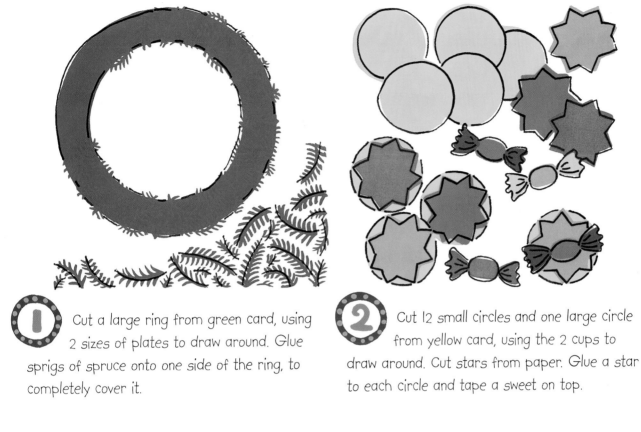

1 Cut a large ring from green card, using 2 sizes of plates to draw around. Glue sprigs of spruce onto one side of the ring, to completely cover it.

2 Cut 12 small circles and one large circle from yellow card, using the 2 cups to draw around. Cut stars from paper. Glue a star to each circle and tape a sweet on top.

3 Using the needle threaded with yarn, make a hole in each yellow card bauble. Tie baubles all the way round the wreath, and finish each with a neat bow.

4 Tie the large bauble from the top of the wreath, so that it hangs in the open center. Hang the wreath from ribbon looped around the top of the wreath and tied in a bow.

CHRISTMAS STOCKING

you will need...

Blue, green, red, yellow, white +
   orange felt, scraps
Fabric scraps in bright colors,
   plaids or checks
Red + green braid ('rickrack') or
   ribbon, scraps
Assorted small buttons
Red + green yarn, scraps
Embroidery floss
Sewing thread
Pins
Needles
Pinking scissors
Scissors
Fabric glue

Hang your stocking up
on Christmas Eve using a loop
of braid sewn inside the top
of the stocking.

Glue a yarn fringe
onto the scarf, then sew
or glue the snowman's
eyes, buttons, scarf and
pompom in place.

Your neat
stitches in bright-
colored thread
will be part of the
decoration.

Glue a pile of
felt snowballs
near the base of
the snowman.

Cut around the
stocking with pinking
scissors to prevent the
edges fraying.

making a Christmas stocking...

 Cut out the pieces for 2 stocking shapes from the colored felt and fabric (trace the stocking on page 254). Cut an extra toe and heel from fabric.

 Glue (or pin, tack and then sew) the pieces together to make 2 stocking shapes. Glue on the toes and heels. Glue or sew on braid or ribbon for decoration.

 From felt, cut a snowman and snowballs (white), scarf (red), hat (yellow) and carrot nose (orange) – trace the picture on page 108. Glue or sew the snowman and snowballs to the front of the stocking. Make a scarf fringe and pompom (see page 250) from yarn. Embroider white snowflakes (see page 247).

Pin the 2 stocking pieces together, right sides out. Trim the edges with pinking scissors. Sew the pieces together using a simple running stitch (see page 247), leaving the top open. Sew a loop of braid inside the top of the stocking so that you can hang it up.

TREE FAIRY

you will need...

Thin colored card, about 40 cm
  (16 in) square
Colored paper, a small sheet
Silver card, about 15 x 30 cm
  (6 x 12 in)
4 popsicle sticks
Assorted tiny beads or
  buttons + sequins
Star stickers
Yellow, orange or brown
  tissue paper, thin
  strips
Felt scrap
Cocktail stick
Dinner plate
Gold thread
Embroidery floss
Embroidery needle
Color markers
Scotch tape
Scissors
Pinking scissors
Glue

Glue the wand onto
the stick hand.

You can sew the
button eyes onto the
card face if you wish.

Make the fairy's
dress and wings
sparkle with lots of
shiny stars and
sequins.

Stitch a short piece of paper string to
the shoe, and unravel both ends to make a
different kind of bow.

making a tree fairy...

1 Cut a semicircle from card with pinking scissors (draw round a dinner plate). Make the semicircle into a cone (see page 246) and tape to hold. Cut the top off the cone.

2 Cover 2 popsicle stick arms with folded colored paper to make the sleeves, leaving the hands peeking out. Glue the arms onto the back of the cone.

3 Fold the silver card in half. Draw a wing on the card, cut it out and open. You will have a pair of wings joined in the middle. Decorate with stars and sequins. Glue to the back of the cone.

4 Cut a head and neck from card (copy the picture above). Draw on a nose and mouth. Glue on bead or button eyes, and tissue paper hair. Thread beads or sequins together for a halo and glue in place. Tape the neck inside the cone.

5 Decorate 2 popsicle stick legs with color markers. Glue on 2 felt shoes (copy the shoes on page 110). For the bows, make a stitch with embroidery floss, knot the ends and fray. Glue the legs inside the front of the cone.

6 For the fairy's wand, glue one end of a length of gold thread to the tip of the cocktail stick. Wind the thread up the stick, covering it. Glue a star or sequin to the top. Decorate the fairy's dress with sequins and stars.

FINGERPRINT ROBIN CARDS + TAGS

you will need...

For the Robin Cards
White + red thin card, large sheets
Green paper, small sheet
Black marker
Red + brown paints
Red + green round stickers
Scissors
Pinking scissors
Glue

For the Robin Tags
White + green thin card, large sheets
Red + green embroidery floss
Red + green round stickers
Red + green colored paper
Red + brown paints
Hole punch
Scissors
Pinking scissors
Glue

Cut strips of colored paper with pinking scissors and glue them as a frame around a group of robins.

Print the robins at random - some standing alone, some in pairs, and some in groups.

Don't try to make all the robins the same – instead draw their beaks and legs facing different ways, and make each one unique!

making a robin card + tag...

Card

1 Dip your index finger into the brown paint and print a robin body onto a large sheet of white card. Dip your little finger in red paint and print a red breast slightly overlapping the body. Print lots of robins.

2 Draw in a *beak*, 2 eyes and 2 legs on each robin with *black* marker.

Tag

3 Cut and fold the white card to make a Christmas card, or cut out a robin and glue it to a folded piece of red card. Decorate with *stickers* and colored paper shapes.

1 Make robins as in Steps 1 and 2 above. Cut tags from the printed white card, or cut out a group of robins and glue onto a tag cut from green card. Decorate the tags with stickers and colored paper. Loop thread through a hole punched in the tag.

CHRISTMAS FUN

113

PAINTED PASTA GARLAND + STAR

you will need...

For the Garland

Pasta-tubes suitable for threading
Paints
Paintbrushes
Color markers
Yarn or embroidery
   floss in bright
   colors
Stiff card, about
   3 x 7 cm
   (1¼ x 2¾ in)
Yarn needle
Scissors

For the Star

8 pasta tubes
Thin colored card, about
   5 cm (6 in) square
Yarn, about 20 cm (8 in)
Paints
Paintbrushes
Button
Scissors
Glue

You can make this garland as long as you like – just keep threading pasta and tying tassels!

Hang the star from a loop of yarn.

When you have finished your garland, tie the yarn ends together or tie each one around the last pasta shape.

making a garland + star...

1 Paint half the pasta tubes red and half green. Allow to dry.

2 Decorate the pasta with spots, wavy lines, zigzags and stripes, using paints or color markers.

3 For the tassels, wind yarn 4 times round the card. Cut off the extra yarn.

Star

4 Thread the needle with another length of yarn and push it between the card and the yarn wound onto it. Repeat and pull this stitch tight. Knot the yarn close to the card, leaving long ends. Cut the yarn along the bottom edge of the card (see page 249).

5 Thread the pasta tubes and tie the tassels onto a long length of yarn.

6 Decorate the pasta as in Steps 1 and 2 above. Glue the pasta onto the card to form a star shape. Glue the button in the center. Trim the card around the star. Glue a loop of yarn to the back of the card to hang it up with.

RAFFIA REINDEER + STRAW STAR

Try and match the twigs for size, shape and number of branches.

The straw star makes a simple decoration which will look festive on the Christmas tree, or hanging from a picture frame or doorway.

Bend the neck, head and tail into shape to give your reindeer personality!

Why not make a whole team of reindeer, linked with thread harnesses, and then start on a sled?

you will need...

You may have to adjust the legs a little at first, but then the reindeer should stand without support.

For the Raffia Reindeer

Natural raffia

Narrow cardboard tube

4 pipe cleaners or chenille stems

Red embroidery floss

2 branched twigs of similar size

Scotch tape (optional)

Scissors

Glue

For the Straw Star

Straw, 4 lengths each about 6 cm (2³⁄₈ in)

Red embroidery floss

Scissors

making a reindeer + star...

Reindeer

Dotted red line indicates the pipe cleaner beneath the raffia.

1 Wind the raffia around the cardboard tube to completely cover it, gluing the raffia on as you go.

2 For the legs, tie lengths of raffia to both ends of 2 pipe cleaners with thread. Make sure the pipe cleaners are completely covered. Fold each in half. Glue the folds to the tube, front and back.

3 Cover another pipe cleaner with raffia. Fold the bundle in half - the fold will be the nose. Bend to make a head and neck. Tie thread around the nose and the top of the neck. Glue the base of the neck to the tube.

Straw Star

4 Cut a pipe cleaner in half. Bundle raffia around one half and tie both ends with thread. Glue one end to the end of the body to make a tail.

5 Glue on twig antlers. Stuff the tube with raffia to finish the body.

1 Make a cross with 2 pieces of straw and tie it at the center with thread (do not cut the thread yet). Lay a second straw cross over the first one to form a star. Bind the crosses together and make a loop of thread to hang the star up with.

POTATO STAMP GIFT WRAP

To get a clear print, press the potato print down cleanly – try not to move it! – and then carefully lift it off.

Print a star made from a freehand drawing for a real handmade look – or design a print of your own.

These Christmas trees are printed in two stages – first the green tree shape, and then the red rectangle for the pot.

The blue dots are printed with a pencil eraser tip dipped in blue paint.

you will need...

For the Star Gift Wrap

Potato, cut in half

White or colored paper, a large sheet

Red + green paint + paintbrushes

Pencil, with eraser tip

Tracing paper

Craft Knife (be careful!)

Pins

Scissors

118

making the gift wrap...

Star

1 On paper, draw a star. Cut out. Pin the paper star to one half of the potato.

2 Cut around the star with a craft knife (an adult should help you with this) about 0.5 cm (¼ in) deep. Cut away the potato around the star.

3 Dip the star into the red paint and print 3 or 4 star shapes onto the wrapping paper. Repeat until you have printed stars all over the paper.

4 Dip the eraser tip of the pencil in green paint and print dots between the stars, all over the paper. Dip the pencil in the paint after every 3 or 4 prints.

119

RAINY DAY
fun with paper

Panda Paper Doll

Curled Paper
Animals

Car Collage
Pinboard

Pencil Holders

Fruity Picture
Frames

PANDA PAPER DOLL

you will need...

Thin card, a large sheet
Cardboard box lid, shoe box-sized
   or smaller
Paper, a large sheet
Paints
Paintbrushes
Color
   markers
Round blue
   stickers
Scotch
   tape
Scissors
Glue

Trace this Panda, or make yours bigger – just be sure the clothes you make fit him!

Don't forget to include tabs with every item of clothing.

making a panda paper doll...

1 Draw a Panda on card (trace the one opposite), making 2 tabs extend below the feet. Paint it black and white. Add stickers for eyes. Cut it out.

2 Cut 2 slits in the box lid to match the position of the feet. Decorate the lid with paint or color marker.

3 Push the tabs on the feet through the slits in the lid. Fold them back under the lid and glue or tape them down. The Panda should now stand upright.

4 Draw Panda's clothes on paper (or trace the ones opposite). Remember the tabs! Paint the clothes or use color markers, and cut out.

5 Fold the tabs back where they join the clothes (see picture above).

6 Dress the Panda in a whole wardrobe of outfits by folding the tabs behind the body to hold the clothes in place.

CURLED PAPER ANIMALS

Starting at the back, overlap black-and-white zigzag tissue strips as spines.

The Hedgehog's feet are cut out and glued on separately.

Make Squirrel's tail really bushy by covering the paper tail with lots of tissue curls.

Add nose, ear, arm and leg details with color markers.

you will need...

For the Squirrel

Thin colored card, a large sheet

Brown paper, about 25 x 30 cm (10 x 12 in)

Paints + paintbrushes

Red, brown, yellow + green tissue paper

Color markers

Pencil

Ruler

Scissors

Pinking scissors

Glue

making a paper animal...

Squirrel

1 Cut out a squirrel from paper using pinking scissors for the back and tail. Glue onto card. Add a nose and eye with color markers.

2 Cut strips of red and brown tissue, each about 7 x 20 cm (2³/₄ x 8 in). Fold the strips in half, lengthways. Cut a zigzag down one long edge.

3 To make curls, pull each point on the strips of tissue paper firmly between your thumb and the edge of the ruler. Cut the strips into small pieces.

Hedgehog

4 Glue the tissue curls onto the tail, mixing the reds and browns. Glue on narrow strips of yellow tissue paper for whiskers.

5 Glue on a ball of tissue for an eye, and another for an acorn. Cut oak leaf shapes from green tissue and glue in place.

1 The Hedgehog's spines are made from strips of black and white tissue paper, folded together and cut into zigzags down one long edge.

125

CAR COLLAGE PINBOARD

Stick the cars onto the card so that 2 are facing one way, and 2 the other.

The strips of yellow paper look like road markings.

you will need...

Cork pinboard

Thin card, about 20 x 30 cm
    (8 x 12 in)

Blue + yellow paper, small sheets

Assorted colored paper, small sheets

Thumb tacks

8 buttons

String, about the length of the
    pinboard

Small notebook + pencil

Scissors

Glue

making a collage pinboard...

1 Cut the thin card into 4 pieces, each measuring about 10 x 15 cm (4 x 6 in).

2 Cut out 4 paper cars, each a different color. Glue a car on each piece of card. Stick 2 blue paper windows on each car.

3 Glue or sew 2 button wheels onto each car.

4 Pin a piece of card in each corner of the pinboard with thumb tacks. Make 2 cars face one way and 2 cars the other way.

5 Cut strips of yellow paper about 1.5 cm (½ in) wide. Cut the strips into 5 cm (2 in) lengths. Glue them around the edge of the board, spacing them evenly.

6 Tie string to the end of the pencil. Make a loop in the free end of the string and pin it to the board. Pin on a notebook too.

FUN WITH PAPER

127

PENCIL HOLDERS

you will need...

For the Ocean Liner Pencil Holder

3 cardboard tubes, from toilet paper

2 cardboard boxes, one shoe box
   and one smaller

Dark blue paper, a small sheet

Colored reinforcement rings
   or round stickers

Paints

Paintbrushes

Aluminum + gold foil, scraps

Yarn, about 40 cm (16 in)

Scotch tape

Fabric, a scrap

Barbecue

skewer

Scissors

Glue

For this pencil holder, glue tubes of different sizes together, glue them onto a base of card, and glue on stars cut from giftwrap.

Use color markers to add details to the port holes, anchor and fish.

making a pencil holder...

Ocean Liner

 1 Paint the tubes red, the small box blue, and the shoe box dark blue with a wavy green sea around its base.

 2 Stick rows of reinforcement rings along the sides of the boxes for port holes. Glue a band of dark blue paper around the top of each red funnel.

 3 Cut fish out of aluminum foil, and an anchor out of gold foil. Glue the fish on below the waves. Tie wool onto the anchor. Tape the end inside the small box.

 4 Tape the funnels inside the small box, then glue this box inside the shoe box. Glue a fabric flag to the top of the skewer. Tape the skewer inside the shoe box.

FUN WITH PAPER

129

FRUITY PICTURE FRAMES

Make sure your photo is the right size for the frame – cut it slightly bigger than the square of card.

Make a fruit salad of Strawberry, Lemon and Cherry frames to display photos of family or pets.

The Cherry frame makes an ideal displa for the photos of twins!

you will need...

For the Apple Frame

Corrugated or plain cardboard, about 30 cm (12 in) square

Newspaper, cut into strips

Raffia or yarn, about 30 cm (12 in)

Paints, paintbrushes + color markers

Scotch tape

Scissors + hole punch

Glue, diluted with water

making a fruity frame...

Apple

1 Draw an apple shape on the cardboard. Cut it out. Cut a square out of the center.

2 Paste newspaper strips on the apple with dilute glue and a paintbrush. Cover the whole surface and the edges. Allow to dry.

3 Punch a hole in the *stalk*. Paint the apple, leaves and stalk, adding leaf markings with color markers. Remember to paint the *back* of the frame too.

4 Tie a loop of raffia through the hole. Place a photo in the frame. Replace the square you cut out and tape it to the frame behind the photo.

RAINY DAY
fun with paint

Matchbox Insect

Printed Crocodile Family

Mosaic Plant Pots

Fingerprint Owl

Stenciled T-Shirts

MATCHBOX INSECT

you will need...

For the Ladybug

Dark brown or black thick paper,
  a small sheet

Matchbox

Pebble, to fit inside matchbox

Paints

Paintbrushes

2 small beads

Button

Straw, a handful

Scissors

Glue

Mixing the paint with the glue makes it stick to the pebble.

Glue the legs slightly under the pebble, making sure they stick out at the sides.

Bee's wings are cut from cellophane, but you could use shiny candy wrappers or tracing paper instead.

The Seashore Beasties have tiny shells glued onto their backs, and scraps of dried seaweed glued on for tails.

making a matchbox insect...

Ladybug

 Mix a little red and black paint with glue. Paint the pebble red. Allow to dry. Paint black spots and a black stripe down the middle.

 Cut 8 small strips of paper, each about 0.5 x 1.5 cm ($^1/_8$ x $^1/_2$ in). Glue on 6 strips for legs and 2 for the antennae. Thread or glue a bead on each antenna.

 Paint the matchbox blue. Allow to dry. Add the flower and wavy line/dot detail.

 Glue the button onto the drawer. Fill the drawer with straw for bedding.

PRINTED CROCODILE FAMILY

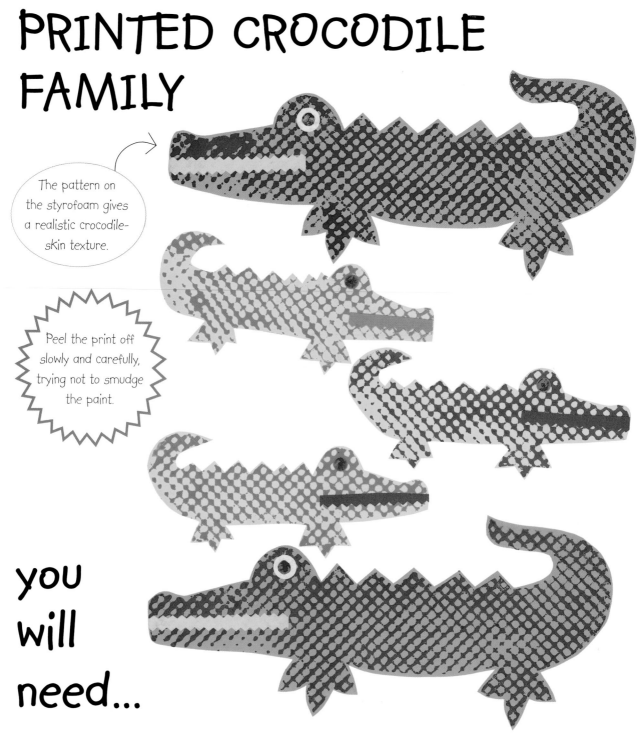

The pattern on the styrofoam gives a realistic crocodile-skin texture.

Peel the print off slowly and carefully, trying not to smudge the paint.

you will need...

Styrofoam, or backing from
    2 large frozen pizzas
Green + yellow thin card,
    large sheets
Yellow, blue or purple paper,
    a small sheet
Green + brown paint

Paintbrushes
Craft knife (be careful!)
Round stickers
Tracing paper
Pencil, with eraser tip
Scissors + pinking scissors
Glue

making a crocodile family...

1 Trace one large and one small crocodile from the picture opposite, or draw your own.

2 Transfer the tracing onto the flat side of the styrofoam (not the patterned side). Cut out the crocodiles with a craft knife (an adult should help you).

3 Dab paint onto the patterned side of the styrofoam crocodile. Make sure the paint is sticky, and not too runny.

4 Press the painted side of the crocodile onto the colored card. Press firmly with your hand – try not to move the crocodile! Carefully peel it off. Print crocodiles all over the card. Allow to dry.

5 Cut out the prints. Give each a sticker eye. Dip the eraser end of the pencil in paint and print a dot on each eye. Cut strips of paper with pinking scissors and glue on for mouths.

6 To make a crocodile stand, fold a rectangle of card (copy the picture above) and glue it on the unpainted side. Fold the feet away from the body on the painted side.

FUN WITH PAINT

137

MOSAIC PLANT POTS

you will need...

For the Primula Pot

Clay plant pot

6 egg shells, crushed

Purple, light green + blue paint

Paintbrushes

Glue, diluted with water

Glue

Arrange the colored egg shells at random, or in a simple pattern, like this one.

Choose your favourite colors, but use a dark color for the pot, and contrasting colors for the egg shells.

Glue the egg shells close enough together to look like mosaic tiles, but leave a gap around each piece for the background color to show through.

making a mosaic plant pot...

Primula

 1 Paint the outside of the clay pot purple. Allow to dry.

2 Paint half the egg shell pieces green, and half blue.

 3 Glue egg shell pieces all round the pot, mixing the blue and green pieces evenly. Leave gaps so that the purple shows through.

 4 Paint the dilute glue all over the outside of the pot. This seals the egg shell layer and acts as a varnish.

FUN WITH PAINT

139

FINGERPRINT OWL

you will need...

Brown + yellow thin card, each
  about 30 cm (12 in) square
Raffia + string, each
  about 50 cm (20 in)
Pale yellow/cream +
  brown paint
Paper fasteners
Brown paper + fabric
  scraps
Bead
Sponge
Yarn needle
Hole punch
Scissors
Pinking scissors
Glue

Hang the Owl from a tree or from your finger using this loop of raffia.

Large buttons would make good eyes.

Cut out the wings so that they are slightly bigger than the handprints.

Pull the Owl's tail and make his wings flap up and down.

making a fingerprint owl...

1 Draw an owl body on brown card. Dip your fingertip in yellow paint and make fingerprints all over the body. Cut out the body.

2 Sponge brown paint onto your hands and make prints on the yellow card. Cut around the 4 fingers of each hand print (leave off the thumb print).

3 With a needle, make 2 holes in the body and one in each wing. Fix the wings to the body with paper fasteners. Punch a hole in the top of the head and loop a piece of raffia through it.

4 Punch a hole in the top of each wing. With the wings down, loop raffia through the holes and knot it, leaving a tail dangling below the body. Knot a bead on the end of this.

5 For each eye, glue a coil of string on a 3 cm (1¼ in) square of paper. Cut round the coil with pinking scissors. Glue in place.

6 Cut a beak from a scrap of fabric and 2 feet from paper (copy the picture opposite). Glue in place on the owl.

STENCILED T-SHIRTS

you will need...

For the Two Big Fish T-shirt

T-shirt

Thin card, about 10 x 20 cm
 (4 x 8 in)

Cardboard, about 10 x 20 cm
 (4 x 8 in)

2 small buttons or beads

Pencil, with eraser tip

Fabric paints

Sponge

Masking tape

Paper towel

Sewing thread

Needle

Scissors

Stencil a school of smaller fish in brilliant colors and brighten up a boring T-shirt.

Make sure that you place the striped stencil exactly over the fish before you begin to dab on the paint, other-wise the stripes will go beyond the outline of the fish.

Use as little paint as possible - the sponge should be almost dry - to prevent the paint creeping under the stencil and giving an untidy outline.

making a stenciled t-shirt...

Two Big Fish

1 Draw a *big* fish on thin card. Cut out and throw away the fish shape, leaving the fish stencil (*see page 251*).

2 Place the stencil on the front of the T-shirt and tape it in position. Slide the cardboard inside the T-shirt, under the stencil.

3 Dip the sponge in *blue* paint and dab it onto a paper towel to remove excess paint. Dab the paint on the stencil. Allow to dry before carefully lifting the stencil.

4 Tape the stencil down on the T-shirt again, this time facing a different way (don't forget to move the card inside the T-shirt!). Repeat Step 3, using green paint.

5 For a striped fish, draw the fish on card as before, but cut out only the stripes. Tape this stencil over a stenciled fish. Dab on paint. For dots, dip a pencil end in paint and print.

6 Sew on buttons or beads for the eyes of both fish.

FUN WITH PAINT

143

RAINY DAY
fun with boxes

Toadstool House

Doll's House

Doll's House
Furniture

Miniature Theater

Clothes Pin
Actors

TOADSTOOL HOUSE

you will need...

Thin card, 3 pieces:

one about 30 cm (12 in) square

one about 10 cm x 15 cm

(4 x 6 in)

one about

15 x 75 cm

(6 x 30 in)

Paints

Paintbrushes

Color markers

Fabric scraps

Scissors

Stapler or glue

The pitch of the roof can be steep or shallow and the house tall or squat, depending on the size of the card cone and base that you make.

Glue a short length of yarn to one end of the spool for the mouse's tail.

Make the door big enough for the mice to go in and out.

To make a mouse, glue one end of a spool with a cut-out of a face of a mouse.

To make the feeding bowl, glue corn kernels to an upturned lid.

making a toadstool house...

1 Cut a circle from the card (draw round a dinner plate). Cut in from the edge to the center. Paint the circle red with yellow spots. Staple or glue it into a cone shape.

2 Cut a sprig of leaves and acorns from the card (copy the picture above). Color them with color markers or paint. Glue the stalk inside the cone.

3 Cut the card rectangle to fit under the perimeter of the roof. Cut an arch for a door. Paint around the arch and add windows, flowers and grass.

4 Staple or glue the base of the house into a cylinder shape. Put the roof on top. Make blankets for the mice from small rectangles of fabric.

FUN WITH BOXES

147

DOLL'S HOUSE

you will need...

2 cardboard boxes of equal size
Patterned giftwrap or wallpaper
White paper, small sheets
Colored paper, small sheets
Fabric scraps
Matchbox, outer shell
Paints
Paintbrushes
Color markers
Scotch tape
Scissors
Glue

You may prefer to paint the outside of the box before you glue on the windows and door.

Make a doorknob and letter box from yellow stickers, with details in color marker.

making a doll's house...

 Cut the flaps off one box to make the house. Glue patterned paper on the walls inside.

 Paint the ceiling (top) and floor (bottom) inside the box.

 Draw or paint an exterior door and 2 windows on colored paper. Cut out. Glue onto the outside of the house.

 Draw or paint a door on colored paper and 2 windows on white paper. Cut out. Glue scraps of fabric to the windows for curtains. Glue the windows and door inside the house.

 Cut 2 sides off the second box, leaving a corner for the roof. Paint this red and add roof tiles with a color marker. Glue on 2 doves cut from white paper.

 Paint the matchbox orange. Cut V-shaped notches in one end so that it fits on the roof as a chimney. Tape the matchbox to the roof to hold it down.

FUN WITH BOXES

149

OLL'S HOUSE FURNITURE

You will need...

For the Table + Stools

2 corks, cut in half
Large empty cotton reel
Fabric scraps
Pencil
Scissors
Glue

For the Chest of Drawers

3 matchboxes
Paints + paintbrushes
3 paper fasteners
Yarn needle
Glue

For The Mirror + Pictures

Scrap of thin card
Aluminum foil
Paints
Paintbrushes
Color markers
Scissors
Glue

Glue the pictures and mirror to the walls of the doll's house and draw the picture wire and nail with a color marker.

For the Bookshelf

White paper, small sheet
Paints + paintbrushes
Color markers
Scissors
Glue

Draw some of the books lying down, or leaning to one side, for a realistic bookshelf.

For the Bed

Matchbox
Scrap of thin card
Paints + paintbrushes
Fabric scraps
Scissors
Glue

For the Rug

Fabric, about 5 x 11 cm
   (2 x 4½ in)
Pin
Glue

making the doll's furniture...

Table + Stools

Glue a fabric cover on the uncut end of each cork (draw round the corks for the right size). Glue a larger fabric circle to the cotton reel as a table cloth.

Chest of Drawers

Glue the matchboxes together. Decorate with paint and color markers. For each drawer, make a hole in the center with the needle, push a paper fastener through and fix inside.

Mirror + Pictures

Cut an oval from card and paint it. Glue a smaller foil oval in the center for a mirror. Draw tiny pictures on squares of card and paint frames around them.

Bookshelf

On paper, draw a shelf with books. Paint and draw in the details. Cut out and glue in position.

Bed

Cut 2 bed ends from thin card. Glue them to the ends of the matchbox. Paint the bed. Glue fabric rectangles on the bed as a pillow and blanket.

Rug

Fray the piece of fabric at both ends with a pin. Glue onto the floor of the doll's house.

MINIATURE THEATER

you will need...

Cardboard box,
  lid flaps cut off
Thin card,
  2 pieces slightly
  smaller than the
  back of the box
4 lids or blocks,
  at least 3 cm
  (1¼ in) deep
Color markers
Gold or silver
  marker pen
Paints
Paintbrushes
Gold star stickers
Gold or aluminum foil
Fabric scraps
2 garden canes
Scotch tape
Scissors
Glue

Make false drapes from scraps of dark fabric and glue on tiny tie-backs to keep them open.

Turn to page 154 to find out how to make these magnetic clothes pin actors.

The actors move when you slide the wooden spoons (and their magnets) about under the theater.

The scenes are suspended from garden canes.

Draw scenes from your favorite fairy tales, or your own stories.

making a miniature theater...

1 Cut a rectangle out of one side of the card-board box for a stage opening (copy the picture above for the correct position).

2 Cut two V-shaped notches in the top of each side of the stage opposite each other. For the feet, glue a lid under each corner.

3 Paint the walls and floor of the theater green. Paint the back wall dark blue, to make a night sky. Stick on star stickers and a foil moon.

4 Paint the outside of the box red and the stage opening border purple. Above the stage add a gold foil crown and detail with gold pen.

5 Glue on fabric drapes and glue on small fabric tie-backs to keep them open.

6 Draw or paint 2 scenes on the card. Glue or tape each scene to a garden cane. The canes rest on the notches cut in the sides of the box.

FUN WITH BOXES

153

CLOTHES PIN ACTORS

you will need...

For the King, Fairy, Woman + Wolf

4 old-fashioned wooden clothes pins

8 magnets

4 wooden spoons

Paints

Paintbrushes

Yellow tissue paper,
   thin strips

Brown, yellow + orange
   yarn scraps

Color markers

Gold marker pen

Fabric or felt scraps

Braid, sequins, star stickers

Brown paper, foil, thin card, scraps

Straw, brush bristles

Matchstick

Embroidery floss
   Needle

Hacksaw
   (be careful!)

Scissors

Glue

Glued-on bits of unraveled string give the Wolf's coat a coarser texture.

The Woman's straw and card broom has hairbrush bristles.

For a drawstring, gather the long edge of a rectangle of fabric using an embroidery needle and floss, ease the gathers around the neck and tie the thread ends in a bow.

The Fairy's matchstick wand has 2 sticker stars glued on back-to-back.

For the King, glue on a yarn beard, a foil crown (you can trace this one), and a fabric cloak fastened with a sequin.

Use a long handled wooden spoon with a magnet to move the actors on and off stage.

making the clothes pin actors...

1 Saw each pin in half, just above where it splits into 2 (an adult should help you with this). Glue a magnet to the base of the top half.

2 For people, draw or paint faces and bodies on the pins. Glue on yarn or tissue for hair, and braid or sequins for decoration. Glue or tie on a fabric cloak or dress.

3 For the wolf, paint the pin brown. Draw eyes, nose and mouth with a color marker. Glue on brown paper ears, wisps of yarn for hair and whiskers, and long strands for a tail.

4 Glue a magnet on each spoon. Make sure it is the correct way up to attract the magnet on its pin character. Decorate the handles with a color marker.

FUN WITH BOXES

155

RAINY DAY
fun with fabric

Seaside
Pin-cushions

Fat Cat Door Stop

Elephant
Wall hanging

Felt Bookmarks

Pajama Bag

SEASIDE PIN-CUSHIONS

you will need...

For the Fish Pin-cushion

Fabric, about 25 x 30 cm
   (10 x 12 in)
Dried pulses (such as lentils) or beans
Braid ('rickrack'), a scrap
Paper, a small sheet
2 buttons
Sewing thread
Pinking scissors
Scissors
Needle
Pins

The Starfish has button eyes and a smile sewn on one side before the 2 star shapes are sewn together.

Make your stitches small and close together to stop the pulses from escaping!

The Crab's legs and pincers are strips of fabric, caught into the stitching when the body pieces are sewn together.

making a seaside pin-cushion...

Fish

1 Make a paper pattern of a fish. Fold the fabric in half and pin the paper pattern to it. Cut out round the pattern with pinking scissors.

2 You will have 2 fabric fish pieces. Sew a button eye on each.

3 Pin the fish pieces together, right sides out. Sew them together using small running stitches, about 0.5 cm (1/4 in) from the edge (see page 247). Leave the tail open.

4 Stuff the fish with pulses - don't make it too full! Sew the tail closed. Sew or glue the braid on the tail for decoration.

159

FAT CAT DOOR STOP

you will need...

Patterned fabric, about 30 x 50 cm (12 x 20 in)

Hessian, 2 pieces 10 cm (4 in) wide x the width of a door

Broad ribbon, about 1.25 m (1¼ yd)

Kapok or old pantyhose

Plain fabric, a scrap

Paper, a scrap

String, a scrap

Yarn needle

Pins

Sewing thread

2 buttons

Pencil

Scissors

Pinking scissors

To sew the mouth and whiskers in one go, start by pushing the needle into the fabric where you want one whisker, come out at the mouth, make 3 stitches, and finish by bringing the needle out at the other whisker.

Cutting the fabric with pinking scissors prevents it from fraying.

Make your stitches small and close together, to stop the stuffing from leaking out.

making a fat cat door stop...

1 Make a paper pattern of a cat. Fold the fabric in half, and pin on the paper pattern. Cut out round the pattern with pinking scissors.

2 On one cat shape, sew button eyes and glue on a fabric nose. Thread the yarn needle with string and sew on a mouth and whiskers. Fray the ends of the whiskers.

3 Pin the 2 cat shapes together, right sides out. Sew them together using small running stitches (see page 247). Leave a small gap at the *base* for the stuffing to fit through.

4 Stuff the cat with kapok. Use the end of a pencil to push the stuffing into the ears. Sew the gap closed.

5 Sew the strips of hessian together along 3 sides (2 long and one short). Stuff the tail through the open end. Fray the *bottom* of the tail. Sew the top end closed.

6 Sew the top of the tail to the side seam of the cat. Sew on a bow made with ribbon where the cat's neck would be.

FUN WITH FABRIC

161

ELEPHANT WALL HANGING

Make a beautifully decorated elephant with plenty of sequins and braid.

These sparkly leaf sequins are a good choice for finishing off the zigzag border.

you will need...

Wooden dowel, 1 cm (½ in) in
    diameter, about 50 cm (20 in) long

Orange, pale orange + blue felt,
    each about 30 cm (12 in) square

Pale blue felt, about 10 cm (4 in)
    square

Lilac felt, about 10 x 30 cm (4 x 12 in)

Braid ('rickrack'), 1.5 m (1½ yd)

Ribbon, scraps

Sewing tape, 5 pieces each about
    10 cm (4 in)

Blue paint + paintbrush

Sewing thread + needle

Assorted sequins + small beads

Paper string or cord, about 1 m (1 yd)

Scissors

Fabric glue

making the wall hanging...

1 From felt, cut an elephant (blue), an ear and a tusk (pale blue), and a saddle and headdress (orange).

2 Glue or sew the elephant onto the background panel of pale orange felt. Glue on the saddle, tusk and headdress.

3 Decorate the elephant, saddle and headdress with sequins, ribbon and braid, glued or sewn on. Decorate the ear and glue it in place.

4 Glue or sew on a large sequin for an eye. For the tail, thread sequins and beads alternately on thread, and sew onto the elephant.

5 Cut a zigzag border in lilac felt to fit across the bottom of the wall hanging. Glue or sew it in place and glue ribbon over the join. Glue or sew braid to the sides and bottom of the wall hanging. Sew a sequin to each point of the zigzag.

6 Sew tape loops to the top of the wall hanging, spacing them evenly. Sew a sequin on each. Paint the dowel blue and slide it through the loops. Tie string at each end of the dowel to hang the picture.

FUN WITH FABRIC

163

FELT BOOKMARKS

you will need...

For the Initials Bookmark

Assorted felt scraps, one at least
   7 x 25 cm (2³/₄ x 9 in)

Small bead or flat button

Paper

Pencil

Fabric glue

Pins

Needle

Sewing thread

Pinking
   scissors

Scissors

Big, bold letters are easier to cut out and more striking.

Make a wiggly Snake with a 'rickrack' tongue and beady eyes.

This racing car has button tire trims and white felt puffs from its muffler.

making a felt bookmark...

Initials

1 Draw the outline of your bookmark, your initials, the star and square on paper. Cut out these paper patterns.

2 Pin the paper patterns to felt scraps of different colors. Cut around the patterns to get the felt shapes you need.

3 Glue the felt letters to the felt bookmark. Glue the square in place, and glue the star over it.

4 Sew a bead or button in the center of the star for decoration.

FUN WITH FABRIC

165

PAJAMA BAG

you will need...

Pillowcase

Fabric scraps, each at least
   10 x 15 cm (4 x 6 in)

Narrow ribbon or cord, about 1.5 m
   (1½ yd)

Paper, a large sheet

Buttons

Pencil

Pins

Needle

Sewing thread

Safety pin

Scissors

Pinking scissors

Fabric glue

Pull the loop at each side to close the bag.

Make the letters big and bold to fill the front of the pillowcase.

Use a star for the dot above the "i", and sew a button on to add a colourful touch.

making a pajama bag...

① Draw the letters for your name or your initials on paper. Draw a star for a dot. Cut out.

② Pin each paper pattern to a scrap of fabric. Cut out the shapes with pinking scissors.

③ Glue the fabric letters to the pillowcase. Make sure the opening of the pillowcase is at the top.

④ Sew around each letter using small running stitches, about 0.5 cm (1/4 in) from the edge (see page 247). Sew a button over any star dots you have used.

⑤ Pin a hem round the opening of the pillowcase, wide enough to take a ribbon. Sew the hem using running stitches, leaving a gap at each side seam.

⑥ Pin a safety pin to one end of the ribbon. Push through the gap into the hem, and thread the ribbon round the pillowcase twice. Sew the ribbon ends together.

167

RAINY DAY
fun with
beads + sequins

Wild Animal Beads

Wild Animal Bracelets

Glitter Necklace
+ Bracelets

Paper + Paper Clip
Pendant

Sequined Room Plaque

Jewelry Box

WILD ANIMAL BEADS

you will need...

Newspaper, torn into strips

Elastic or thread, about 60 cm (24 in)

Glue, diluted with water

Petroleum jelly

4 Knitting needles

Potato, cut in half

Paints

Paintbrushes

30 small wooden
   beads

Varnish

Mix stripes and spots to make a really wild necklace, or stick to the markings of one animal and experiment with color.

Alternate wild animal beads with small wooden beads.

making wild animal beads...

1 Mix the newspaper strips with glue to make papier mâché pulp (*see page 245*). Coat the knitting needles with petroleum jelly.

2 Take marble-sized lumps of papier mâché and mould them round a knitting needle to make small spheres. Leave a gap between each one. Repeat using the other knitting needles until you have enough beads.

3 Stick the knitting needles into the cut potato (don't let the beads touch). Leave them to dry for 5 days. Take the beads off the needles. Allow to dry for another day.

4 Paint the beads a plain color. Allow to dry. Then paint on spots and stripes. Paint on a coat of varnish. Thread the beads onto elastic, alternating with wooden beads.

171

WILD ANIMAL BRACELETS
you will need...

Cardboard tube
Newspaper, torn into strips
Paints
Paintbrushes
Varnish
Glue, diluted with water
Scissors

Clear, bold markings are the most eye-catching.

Paint the inside of the bracelets in a contrasting color.

making a wild animal bracelet...

 1 Cut a 3 cm (1¼ in) ring off the end of the cardboard tube with the scissors.

2 Paste newspaper strips on the ring with dilute glue and a paintbrush. Cover the ring completely several times. Allow to dry.

 3 Paint the bracelet a base color inside and out. Allow to dry.

4 Paint stripes or spots on the outside of the bracelet. Add a coat of varnish.

FUN WITH BEADS + SEQUINS

173

GLITTER NECKLACE + BRACELETS

you will need...

For the Fish Bracelet

Clear plastic tubing, about 20 cm (8 in)

Small lump of plastic or modeling putty

Colored sand, from stores supplying
aquariums

Balsa wood, about
3 x 5 cm
(1¼ x 2 in)

Glitter

Paints

Paintbrushes

Scotch tape

Craft knife
(be careful!)

Embroidery
floss

Jug

Knitting needle

Glue

The necklace is made in
the same way as the bracelet,
only with a longer piece
of tubing.

Fill the tubing
with glitter, sequins, beads,
seeds - even tiny pieces
of candy!

You can bind the tubing
with embroidery floss of
different colors if you like.

GREAT STUFF

making a glitter bracelet...

Fish

1 Cut a piece of tube to fit comfortably round your wrist. Plug one end of the tube with a small lump of putty.

2 Put the sand and glitter into a jug. Fill the tube. Plug the other end with putty.

3 Tape the ends together. Bind the ends with embroidery floss to cover and strengthen the join. Glue as you go.

4 Cut a small fish out of balsa wood (copy the one above). Poke an eye hole with the knitting needle. Paint the fish on both sides. Hang the fish from the bangle with a piece of thread looped through the eye.

FUN WITH BEADS + SEQUINS

175

PAPER + PAPER CLIP PENDANT

you will need...

Assorted colored paper,
small sheets

3 or 4 plastic
drinking straws

Chenille stem or pipe
cleaner, folded
in half

Assorted beads,
about 25

Embroidery floss or
cord, about 1 m (1 yd)

Colored paper clips,
about 25

Scissors

Glue

Simply tie the thread ends together, or make a loop in one end and knot a bead on the other.

Make the necklace as colorful as possible.

Include the bendy part of the straw for added texture.

making a paper clip pendant...

1 For paper beads, cut 20 tall (isosceles) paper triangles in different colors (trace the ones above). Cut the straws into 20 sections about 2-2.5 cm (¾-1 in) long.

2 Spread glue on the back of a triangle. Lay the straw on the base of the triangle and roll it up in the paper. Glue the tip of the triangle to hold it.

3 Push the folded pipe cleaner through a 4 cm (1½ in) piece of straw, cut just below the bend. Push 2 beads onto the fold.

4 Push a bead onto each end of the pipe cleaner and bend the ends open. For each wing, hang 2 linked paper clips from the straw and thread a bead onto one.

5 Push a paper clip into the top of the straw as a hanging link. Glue the paper clips in place inside the straw.

6 Push a bead onto each remaining paper clip. Thread beads and paper clips alternately onto embroidery floss. Hang the pendant from the center. Tie the ends.

SEQUINED ROOM PLAQUE

you will need...

For the Name Plaque

Salt dough (*see page 252*)

Paints + paintbrushes

Sequins, tiny beads

Varnish

Rolling pin

Knife

Ruler

Baking tray

Metal skewer

Colored cord or
embroidery floss,
about 30 cm
(12 in)

The Snail has beads glued all over his body and shell, and his feelers are beads with sequins glued on top.

Paint the plaque in pastel colors, then paint the name and add hearts and patterns in bold, contrasting colors.

Glue tiny beads to the letters of the name, and decorate the border with sequins.

making a room plaque...

1 Roll out the salt dough. Measure out a piece 21 × 30 cm (8¼ × 12 in) using the ruler. Cut it out and place it on a baking tray (see page 252).

2 Roll out long thin sausages of dough. Use these to make an inner and outer border for the plaque. Join short pieces in place. Make a hole in the top 2 corners with the skewer.

3 Roll out more thin sausages to make the letters and the border. Bake the plaque (see page 252). Allow to dry.

4 Paint the plaque. Paint on a coat of varnish. Glue on beads and sequins. Hang the plaque from cord tied at the holes.

JEWELRY BOX

Use lots of sequins, sparkly stars and colored paper shapes, embellished with silver pen, to lavishly decorate the box.

If you don't have a mirror, you could use an oval of foil to decorate the centre of the lid.

you will need...

Cardboard box, shoe box-sized
Purple and blue paint + paintbrushes
Small oval mirror
Dark blue, mid blue + green paper, small sheets
Thick aluminum foil
Dry ballpoint pen

Stickers, sequins
Color markers, silver marker pen
Embroidery floss in 3 colors or ribbon, about 60 cm (24 in)
Old key
Scissors, pinking scissors
Glue

making a jewelry box...

① Paint the outside of the bottom of the box blue, and the lid purple.

② Cut a diamond from mid blue paper. Glue it in the center of the box lid. Glue the mirror in the center of the diamond.

③ Cut two 6 cm (2³/₈ in) squares of foil in half to make 4 triangles. Draw patterns on the triangles with the ballpoint pen. Glue triangles to the corners of the lid.

④ Glue a strip of green paper to one long side of the lid. Glue on a foil circle, cut with pinking scissors and decorated. Glue on a dark blue paper keyhole.

⑤ Decorate the lid with sequins, stickers, color markers and silver pen. Draw a pattern on the bottom of the box with color markers and silver pen.

⑥ Twist together the 3 colors of embroidery floss to make a cord. Loop the cord through the key and knot the end.

MAKE-BELIEVE
dressing up

Explorer

Pirate

Native American

Knight

Astronaut

183

EXPLORER rainforest

you will need...

Green, blue + yellow paper or
    paper card, large sheets
Thin card in bright colors,
    small sheets
Chenille stems or pipe cleaners,
    colored
Clothes line or string/twine, hung
    between 2 poles or trees
Plastic garden netting
Paints
Paintbrushes
Sponge
Pencil
Color markers
Stickers
Clothes pins or paper clips
Scissors
Pinking scissors
Glue

GREAT STUFF

making a rainforest...

1 Sponge yellow, green and blue paint onto the sheets of paper to make different patterns and textures.

2 Draw leaf shapes on the painted paper with a pencil. Cut out the leaves.

Butterfly

3 Decide on the animals that will inhabit your rainforest. You may want to add to my collection of birds, butterflies, frogs and snakes.

4 Fold a sheet of yellow card in half. Draw half a butterfly on one side. Cut out. You will have a pair of wings joined in the middle.

and the animals...

Bird

5 Fold a pipe cleaner in half and push the fold down a 3 cm (1 1/4 in) piece of straw. Decorate the wings with stickers.

6 Cut a bird body and wing from *blue* card. Paint a *beak*, an *eye* and feather details on the body, and feathers on the wing.

Lemur

7 Cut the lemur and tail from brown card. Add sticker eyes. Draw in a nose and a mouth and add arm and leg details with color markers.

8 Hang the netting over the clothes line. Pin or clip the foliage, flowers and forest creatures to the netting. Clip some foliage to the back of the netting too, for added depth.

DRESSING UP

187

EXPLORER compass + binoculars

you will need...

For the Compass

Coffee jar lid

Red + green colored paper,
  small sheets

Color markers

Crayons

Scissors

Paper fastener

Yarn needle

Glue

The zigzag pattern makes the pointers look as if they are trembling, just as real compass needles do.

Gently move the pointers so that they point to differe points of the compass.

For the Binoculars

2 small cardboard tubes

2 larger cardboard tubes,
  paper towel core, cut in half

Paints + paintbrushes

Colored paper, small sheets

Egg carton

Bottle top

Ribbon or tape, about 70 cm (27½ in)

Double-sided tape

Scotch tape

Stapler

Scissors

Glue

Paint or draw focus controls in black and white.

Loop the ribbon over a strap of colored paper and staple onto the tube for a realistic look.

making the compass + binoculars...

Compass

 1 Remove card from lid. Color the card yellow with crayon. Divide the circle into quarters. Mark N (North), S (South), E (East) and W (West) with a color marker.

2 Cut 2 large diamond-shaped pointers from red paper and 2 smaller pointers from green. Draw a zigzag pattern on each pointer with color marker.

3 With the needle, make a small hole through the center of each pointer and the card. Push a paper fastener through the green pointers, then the red, and then the card. Glue back into the lid.

Binoculars

 1 Paint the inside of the larger tubes blue or gray to look like lenses. Glue strips of paper around all 4 tubes to make stripes. Paint black and white focus controls.

 2 Cut 2 rings from the egg carton. Glue them to the openings of the small tubes. Paint the rings black. Stick the bottle top between the small tubes with double-sided tape or glue.

3 Stick the large tubes onto the small tubes with double-sided tape. Staple each end of the ribbon strap to a large tube.

PIRATE hat, beard, eye patch + earring

you will need...

Give the skull a ghoulish grin with black marker pen.

For the Pirate Hat
Thick black paper, about
   45 x 60 cm (18 x 24 in)
White paper, about
   25 x 50 cm (10 x 20 in)
Black marker pen
Stapler
Scissors
Glue

If you have no black paper, cut the hat out of white paper, trace on the skull and crossbones and paint black all except the skull and crossbones.

For the Beard
Thick black paper, about 30 cm
   (12 in) square
Black yarn or raffia or thread
Shirring elastic, about
   75 cm (30 in)
Hole punch
Scissors
Glue

Loop the elastic round your ears to hold the beard in place.

Trim the yarn around the edges of the beard shape and keep the mouth opening clear.

For the Eye Patch + Earring
Thick black paper, about 10 cm (4 in)
   square
Shirring elastic, about 75 cm (30 in)
Curtain ring
Scissors

The eye patch elastic goes over one ear and under the other to hold the patch in place.

making a hat, beard, eye patch + earring...

Hat

 Fold the black paper in half and cut out 2 hat shapes with the scissors. Copy the shape of the hat (see opposite page).

2 Cut out a skull and crossbones from white paper. Glue onto the front of the hat. Add skull features in pen. Staple the 2 hat pieces together at the sides, to fit your head.

Beard

I Cut out a beard shape from the black paper. Cut a smile shape for a mouth. Punch a hole on each side of the beard with the hole punch.

2 Glue on enough yarn to cover the paper beard. Trim around the edges and the mouth. Tie a piece of elastic at each side, and make 2 loops at the ends, to go around your ears.

Eye patch + Earring

I Cut out an eye patch from black paper. Make a small hole at each side and thread elastic through. Tie at the back to fit your head.

2 Tie a piece of elastic to the curtain ring. Make a loop and tie onto the eye patch elastic, so that when you are wearing the eye patch, the earring hangs down next to your ear.

DRESSING UP

191

PIRATE treasure chest

you will need...

Cardboard box, shoe box-sized
Brown paint + paintbrush
Black paper, a large sheet
Metallic crayon, bronze
Paper fasteners
Gold or yellow round stickers
Card disks of
    different
    coin sizes
Aluminum + gold
    foil
Dry ballpoint pen
Black marker pen
Paper clips
Bradawl or
    yarn needle
Scissors
Glue

Fill your chest with gold doubloons, pieces of eight and precious chains you have made, as well as costume jewelry and any other sparkly treasures.

Once you have a chest full of priceless treasure, perhaps you should think about a really secret hiding place - and a treasure map!

The markings on the coins are made by drawing on the foil with a dry ballpoint pen.

making a treasure chest...

1 Paint the box and lid brown to look like wood. Allow to dry.

2 Rub the crayon on the black paper to make it shine. Cut the paper into strips about 3-4 cm (1-1½ in) wide. Glue the strips onto the box to make stripes.

3 Use the bradawl to make holes in the stripes. To make studs, push a paper fastener through each hole and open out on the inside of the box.

4 Draw a keyhole shape (trace the one above) on a gold/yellow sticker in black marker pen. Stick on the front of the box.

5 Wrap card disks in foil or cover on both sides with a gold/yellow sticker. Draw on coin markings with a dry ballpoint pen, or draw on the stickers with color markers.

6 Link together paper clips to make chains of different lengths for necklaces and bracelets.

NATIVE AMERICAN
braided headband + neck purse

you will need...

For the Headband

Black raffia or yarn, cut into 25 cm
  (10 in) lengths
4 colored feathers
Broad ribbon, about 45 cm (18 in)
Braid, about 45 cm (18 in)
Elastic, about 10 cm (4 in)
Assorted colored beads
Embroidery floss, in one or
  2 bright colors
Embroidery needle
Sewing thread
Needle
Scissors
Glue

Hook the tied end of the raffia bunches onto a doorknob or coat hook to hold it still while you braid the raffia.

Sew or glue beads on singly, or sew a string of beads onto the headband.

Catch in a feather or tie on a few beads at the end of the plait.

This purse has a fringe made of strips of ribbon, caught into the bottom seam of the purse.

Bury the end of the embroidery floss by pushing it back into the tightly-wound floss, using the needle.

For the Neck Purse

Felt or fabric, 2 pieces each about
  12 x 16 cm (5 x 6½ in)
Shoelace or narrow ribbon, about
  45 cm (18 in)
Narrow ribbon, a scrap
2 colored feathers

Assorted colored beads
Sewing thread, embroidery floss
Needle, embroidery needle
Scissors
Pinking scissors
Glue

making a headband + purse...

Headband

1 Wind sewing thread around the top ends of 2 bunches of raffia. Braid the raffia. Wind embroidery floss round the bottom ends.

2 Glue braid onto the broad ribbon. Sew elastic onto each end of the ribbon to make a circle which fits round your head.

3 Sew or glue beads onto the headband for decoration. Sew a braid to each side. Finish with 2 feathers, sewn or glued on at the back.

Purse

1 Fold down one piece of felt 4 cm (1½ in) from the top. Cut the fold into an envelope flap shape. This is the back of the purse.

2 Cut a 4 cm (1½ in) fringe on the bottom of the other piece of felt (the front of the purse). Glue or sew on beads and work a row of cross-stitch on either side.

3 Sew the felt pieces on 3 sides. Sew a bead on the front and a ribbon loop on the flap. Knot beads and sew feathers on the shoe lace before sewing it to the purse.

NATIVE AMERICAN totem pole

you will need...

2 old tires

Cardboard boxes of different sizes

Lids, tubes, egg cartons

Acrylic paints in bright colors

Poster paints in bright colors

Paintbrushes

Parcel tape

Stickers

Glue

Owl faces like these are a good example of what can be done with paint, color markers and stickers.

The uglier the face and the fiercer the expression, the better!

Don't forget to decorate your totem pole on all sides.

Practise your most energetic 'rain dance' around a totem pole like this one.

making a totem pole...

1 Paint the tires with acrylic paints. Put one on top of the other. (You may need help with this.)

2 Tape the boxes shut. Paint the boxes in a variety of poster paint colors.

3 Paint funny faces, monster faces and designs on the boxes. Tape or glue on lids, egg cartons and tubes and paint them too, for a 3-D effect. Use stickers for added detail.

4 Tape the boxes together one on top of the other, and paint over the tape. Push the bottom box into the tires to stop the totem pole from falling over.

KNIGHT helmet + tunic

you will need...

For the Helmet

Thick black paper, a large sheet

Metallic crayon, silver

Plastic wall plug

Feathers

Stapler

Paper
    fasteners

Glue

Silver or gold stickers would make bright studs too, or draw them in with marker pen.

If you have no wall plugs, bind the feathers with colour thread and glue on the helmet.

For the Tunic

Fabric or strong paper, 2 pieces each
    about 30 x 50 cm (12 x 20 in)

Fabric in contrasting color,
    about 40 x 60 cm (16 x 24 in)

Fabric tape or bias binding,
    about 80 cm (31½ in)

Stapler

Sewing thread

Needle

Scissors

Glue or fusible web

Draw in the bird's eye details with a colour marker

The bird could also be traced straight onto the tunic and then painted with fabric paint.

making a helmet + tunic...

Helmet

1 Rub the crayon over the black paper to give it a shiny metallic look.

2 Cut a strip of paper 4 x 60 cm (1½ x 24 in). Staple it to fit your head. Cut 2 strips about 4 x 34 cm (1½ x 13½ in). Staple these on side to side and front to back.

3 Cut a noseguard from the paper. Attach it to the helmet with a paper fastener. Decorate the helmet with paper fastener studs.

Tunic

4 Glue feathers into the wall plug. Glue the plug to the top of the helmet.

1 Cut the fabric tape into 4 equal lengths. Staple, sew or glue on 2 pieces as shoulder straps (leave a gap for your head), and the other 2 across the sides.

2 Fold the contrasting fabric in half. Cut 2 bird shapes. Stick one on the front and one on the back of the tunic with glue or fusible web (see page 248).

KNIGHT'S shield

you will need...

Large cardboard box, flattened

Thin card, about 4 x 15 cm
   (1½ x 6 in)

Paints + paintbrushes

Pencil

Color markers

Parcel tape or Scotch tape

Scissors

Copy this castle design for a simple but striking decoration.

The owl, like the falcon and eagle, were symbols of power and bravery.

The fleur de lys is a simplified lily, and was a popular heraldic emblem.

Use colorful paint, marker pens and stickers to decorate your shield.

making a shield...

Fleur de lys

1 Cut the shield shape from the cardboard.

2 Draw the fleur de lys design in pencil on the shield.

3 Paint the fleur de lys and the background. Use color markers to add detail.

4 To make a handle, tape the card to the back of the shield. Make sure the handle is big enough for you to grasp.

201

ASTRONAUT jetpack

The radio is a matchbox painted black and decorated with silver marker pen, stickers and a coiled-wire antenna.

Use your imagination and invent gadgets and gizmos galore. Your jetpack can be whatever color you choose.

The plastic bottles are stuck upside down.

The control panel can be made from cardboard or paper.

you will need...

Large cereal box

Grey + black paint + paintbrushes

2 plastic bottles with tops

Paper or thin card, about
  15 cm (6 in) square

Assorted lids (small jars, bottles)

Styrofoam or frozen pizza backing,
  about 10 x 25 cm (4 x 10 in)

Matchbox

Black + silver marker pens

Silver, black, white, number stickers

Scrap of coiled, thin wire

Small bead

Fabric or webbing, 2 strips each
  about 5 x 50 cm (2 x 20 in)

Aluminum foil

Parcel tape or Scotch tape

Scissors

Glue

making a jetpack...

1 Tape the lid of the cereal box shut. Paint the box gray.

2 Cover the bottles with foil. Glue the bottles onto the box, with tops facing down. Cut 6 strips of paper about 2 x 15 cm (³/₄ x 6 in). Decorate using stickers or silver and black marker pens. Glue a strap over the top, middle and bottom of each bottle.

3 Thread the bead onto the wire. Tape the wire to the matchbox. Glue the matchbox to the top of the box. Paint the matchbox black. Glue a strip of styrofoam between the bottles. Add dials and control buttons with stickers, marker pen, and glued-on painted lids.

4 Tape or glue the fabric strips onto the box so you can wear it like a backpack.

ASTRONAUT robot

you will need...

Assorted cardboard boxes
Assorted cardboard tubes
Assorted lids
Paint, black, silver, red
Paintbrushes
Old rubber gloves
2 plastic bottles (juice
    or bubble bath)
Foam scrap, cut into a
    small circle
Aluminum foil
2 scraps of thin wire,
    coiled
2 beads
White, black, silver + numbered
    stickers
Silver marker pen
Black marker pen
Paper clips
Parcel tape or Scotch tape
Elastic, about 1.5 m (1½ yd)
Scissors
Glue

204

Paint the foam nose red before gluing to the Robot's face.

Make Robot shiny with silver stickers and silver marking pen.

The elastic threaded through the arms gives them movement.

Use lids, tubes, stickers - and your imagination - to make buttons, levers and flashing lights.

Try to match up the size of boxes and tubes on either side.

making a robot...

1 First, sort out the boxes and tubes you will need. Head: a medium-sized box. Arm: a tube and a bottle. Leg: a shoe box (foot), a medium-sized box (calf) and a larger box (thigh).

2 Paint the glove hands black and silver. Cover 2 tubes and 2 bottles with foil. Tie elastic round the wrist of a glove and thread it through a tube and a bottle. Do the same for the other arm.

3 Cover a large box with silver foil. Cut a round hole in each side for the arms to fit tightly into. Tie the elastic from the 2 arms together inside the box. Then tape the box shut.

4 For control buttons, glue lids onto the body. Stick on stickers, silver foil, tubes and paper clips and add details with a marker pen.

5 Cut a hole in the lid of the shoe box for the leg to fit tightly into. Tape the 3 leg boxes together before painting black and silver. Tape the thigh boxes to the body.

6 Paint the head box black. Stick on a foam nose and stickers for eyes and mouth. Add a bead to each wire, tape to the matchboxes. Glue to the head and attach the body.

MAKE-BELIEVE
my second home

Hide

Pirate Ship

Tepee

Castle

Space Rocket

207

HIDE
you will need...

8 bamboo canes, 4 long, 4 shorter
Large piece of fabric, the size of a
    double sheet
Green, yellow or blue
    scraps of crepe
    paper, fabric, felt
    + card
Paints
Paintbrushes
String or twine,
    about 2 m (2 yd)
Pencil
Safety pins
Clothes pins
Pinking scissors
Scissors

Take cover in your hide and watch the exotic birds and animals of the rainforest in secret.

If you have permission, glue the leaves onto the fabric so that you can use your hide again and again.

Choose fabric in a dark color to blend in with the forest.

Try and cover the fabric with leaves of different shapes, colors and textures.

making a hide...

① Push the 4 long canes into the ground to make a square frame. Tie the shorter canes around the top with string.

② Lay the fabric over the frame and pin it onto the canes to hold it in place. Let the edges of the fabric just overlap at the front, to make an entrance.

③ Cut leaves from crepe paper, felt and card with scissors. Cut fabric leaves with pinking scissors. Paint some of the paper and card leaves.

④ Pin the leaves all over the hide with safety pins. Close the entrance with a safety pin or clothes pin, leaving a gap big enough for your binoculars to fit through.

MY SECOND HOME

PIRATE SHIP

you will need...

3 cardboard boxes, 2 medium + one large

Paints + paintbrushes

2 plastic or cardboard tubes

Ping pong balls

Small doll

Black fabric or card, about
   10 x 20 cm (4 x 8 in)

White fabric or paper, about
   10 x 20 cm (4 x 8 in)

3 garden canes

Broom, or just the
   handle

2 pillowcases

Cardboard, about
   10 cm (4 in) square

Ball of string

Hole punch

Craft knife (be careful!)

Yarn needle

Clothes pegs

Stapler

Scissors

Glue

Use paint or color markers to add detail to the ship, the flag, and even, if you have permission, to the pillowcase sails.

If you make flags from black card, glue them to the cane and the mast instead of tying them.

If the box is big enough, you may be able to go aboard your pirate ship

Paint cardboard cannons grey on the inside.

Weigh anchor by pulling on the string inside the ship.

making a pirate ship...

1 Staple the 2 smaller boxes to each end of the large box so that they sit slightly higher than the large box. Paint the ship on all sides.

2 Paint the tubes black. With the craft knife, cut 2 holes in the large box just big enough for the cannons to squeeze through. Paint balls black for cannonballs.

3 Cut an anchor from cardboard and paint black. Punch a hole at the top, tie the string through it. Push the end into a hole in the box and tape down.

4 Make 2 holes in the bow (front) of the ship with the needle. Loop the string round the doll, push the string through the holes and tie the ends together inside the box.

5 Make 2 Jolly Rogers. Punch 2 holes in each. Tie one to a cane with string, and tape to the stern (back) of the ship.

6 Bind 2 canes across the broom handle with string. Pin the pillowcase sails to each side of the mast. Tie the second flag to the top of the mast with string.

TEPEE

you will need...

3 long bamboo canes

String or twine, about 1 m (1 yd)

Large piece of fabric,
   such as an old sheet

Fabric paints + paintbrushes

42 ribbon or fabric tape strips,
   each about 15 cm (6 in) long

Pencil

Sewing thread

Needle

Pinking scissors

Tie colorful ribbon or tape to the top of the tepee as decoration.

Cut the fabric with pinking scissors to prevent it from fraying.

Dress up in your beaded headband and neck purse and invite your friends to a real pow-wow in your tepee.

The tepee is not waterproof, so don't forget to bring it indoors if it rains!

making a tepee...

1 Tightly bind the bamboo canes together at the top with string so they can be opened into a pyramid.

2 Cut 3 identical triangles of fabric with sides the same length as the canes.

3 Cut a slit in one triangle from the centre of the bottom edge to half way up the triangle for the opening flap.

4 Sew a ribbon tie to the top, middle and bottom of each side of the flap (6 in all). Sew 6 ties evenly-spaced on the sides of the 3 triangles (36 in all).

5 Draw a border design in pencil along the bottom of each triangle and the opening flap of the tepee. Paint the border design in bright colors.

6 Push the canes into the ground to make a pyramid shape (you may need help with this). Tie the fabric onto the bamboo frame with the ribbon ties.

213

CASTLE

you will need...

Large cardboard box
4 cardboard tubes, from paper towel
Cardboard, about 15 cm (6 in) square
Card, about 20 x 30 cm (8 x 12 in)
Paints + paintbrushes
4 thin garden canes (no sharp points)
Twine or string, about 40 cm (16 in)

Color markers
Craft knife (be careful!)
Double-sided tape (optional)
Yarn needle
Scissors
Glue

Place the castle on a piece of blue fabric just bigger than the box – and lower the drawbridge over the moat you have made!

Cut flags from colored paper card and add bright stickers for your own design.

Outline the battlements with color marker.

Raise and lower the drawbridge from within the castle by pulling or releasing the twine.

Paint the door blue before adding a black portcullis drawn in marker.

making a castle...

1 With the craft knife, cut notches all round the top of the box. (An adult should help you with this.) Space the notches evenly.

2 In the same way, cut evenly-spaced notches around the top of the 4 cardboard tubes.

3 Glue the tubes to the box (or use double-sided tape), 2 at the front and 2 at the back.

4 Paint the castle in the following colors: red archery slits, blue windows, a red arch over a blue door and a black portcullis.

5 Cut the cardboard to cover the arch. Fold the bottom 1 cm (1/2 in) and glue under the box. Push the needle threaded with twine through the drawbridge and arch and back through the drawbridge. Knot the ends of the twine.

6 Draw and paint 4 flags with a design of your choice on the card. Glue each one onto a cane. Tape one cane to the inside of each tower.

SPACE ROCKET

you will need...

Large grey or white cardboard box, big enough to sit in

2 cardboard tubes

Thin card, about 50 cm (20 in) square

Corrugated cardboard, about 8 × 30 cm (3¼ × 12 in)

Yellow, red, orange colored tissue or cellophane

Paints

Paintbrushes

Stickers

Color markers

Parcel tape

Scotch tape

String

Yarn needle

Scissors

Glue a burst of red, orange and yellow tissue or cellophane 'flames' to the rocket tail and boosters.

Put rows of silver dot stickers or marker pen dots on the booster fins.

Stick round stickers over rectangular stickers to make realisti dials for the control panel.

Paint the inside of the boosters black.

Decorate the rocket nose cone and boosters with paint, marker pens and stickers.

making a space rocket...

 Cut 3 flaps off the box, leaving the front flap for the control panel. Use stickers and color markers to make buttons and dials on the control panel.

 Cut one small and one large semicircle from card. Tape each into a cone shape. Cut the point off the small cone. Cut notches around the bottom of the cones and fold back. Tape the large cone to the front of the box, and the small cone to the back.

3 Paint the tubes to look like boosters. Loop string around the front of each tube, thread through 2 holes in the side of the box, and tie on the inside. Make another loop for the back of each tube.

4 Paint the corrugated card side fins. Glue a fin onto each booster. Tape or glue strips of tissue or cellophane into the boosters and tail of the rocket to look like flames.

217

MAKE-BELIEVE
Puppets

Wiggly Snake
Puppets

Life-size Concertina
Puppets

Finger Puppets

Wooden Spoon
Puppets

Sock Puppets

219

WIGGLY SNAKE puppets

you will need...

For the Tube Snake

Cardboard tubes

Colored paper, a scrap

Paint + paintbrushes

Stickers

String or yarn, about 1 m (1 yd)

2 short sticks or plant canes
   (no sharp points)

2 beads

Yarn needle

Scissors

Glue

The wiggly snake is made from threaded corks.

Have fun painting colorful markings.

Use the sticks to make your snake wriggle.

Beware of sharp points!

To finish, knot the string.

Make a tongue from colored paper or string.

making a wiggly puppet...

Tube Snake

1 Cut up the tubes into rings about 3 cm (1¼ in) long to make the body of the snake. Cut a longer tube for the head.

2 Paint and decorate the tubes inside and out. On the head tube, paint eyes (or use stickers) and glue on a string/paper tongue.

3 Thread the rings onto the string. Using the needle, push the string through the cardboard of the head and tail tubes. Knot the string to keep it there.

4 Glue a bead to one end of each stick. Tie a piece of string to each stick, then tie one string to the head and one string to the tail.

221

LIFE-SIZE CONCERTINA puppets

you will need...

Thin card, about 75 x 70 cm (30 x 27½ in) for face, body, arms and legs

Cardboard, about 36 x 8 cm (14 x 3 in) for shoulders

Colored paper

Paints

Paintbrushes

Stickers

String or yarn

Yarn or raffia

Scotch tape

Color markers

Scissors

Glue or stapler

Draw in freckles with marker pen.

Cut a nose from thin card and glue onto face.

Glue paper to card for this skirt.

Use stickers to add detail and colour.

Push yarn or string laces through a small hole in the card and then tie in a bow.

making a concertina puppet...

1 On a 20 x 60 cm (8 x 24 in) piece of card, paint a jumper and shorts or skirt. Fold the card concertina-style every 5 cm (2 in) down its length.

2 From card, cut out arms with hands (trace round your own) and legs with shoes. Paint and decorate the sleeves, socks and shoes with stickers and marker pen.

3 Cut out a head the same width (20 cm/ 8 in) as the body. Draw on a mouth and use stickers for eyes and cheeks. Glue on paper and yarn or raffia for hair.

4 Glue or staple the legs to the body. Then stick or staple the head, arms and body onto the shoulders. To carry your puppet, tape a loop of string to the back of head.

FINGER puppets
you will need...

For the Leopard Puppet

Orange felt, about 15 cm (6 in) square

Yellow felt, about 7 x 5 cm

(2³/₄ x 2 in)

Black felt, a scrap

2 small buttons

Color marker

Yellow + orange

spot stickers

Chenille stems, pipe

cleaners or straw

Black + yellow sewing

thread

Needle

Pinking scissors

Glue

Use the yellow and orange stickers to make Leopard's spots.

Leopard's mouth has been sewn in black thread using a simple backstitch.

Ladybird's feelers are beads threaded on plastic loops.

Panda has a black and white felt head and a scrap of ribbon just for fun.

Make a crazy Owl with scraps of braid, stickers and a sewn-on paper clip.

making a finger puppet...

Leopard

1 Fold your orange felt in half using pinking scissors, cut 2 pieces.

2 For the face, sew button eyes onto one piece of orange felt, glue on a black felt nose and sew (or draw in with marker pen) a black mouth (see page 247).

3 Put the ears at the top of the head between the 2 pieces of orange felt. Sew the 2 pieces of orange felt together using yellow thread and a running stitch (see page 247).

4 Make leopard spots with stickers or felt pen. Make a tiny slit either side of Leopard's face and thread through pipe cleaners or straw for the whiskers.

PUPPETS

225

WOODEN SPOON puppets

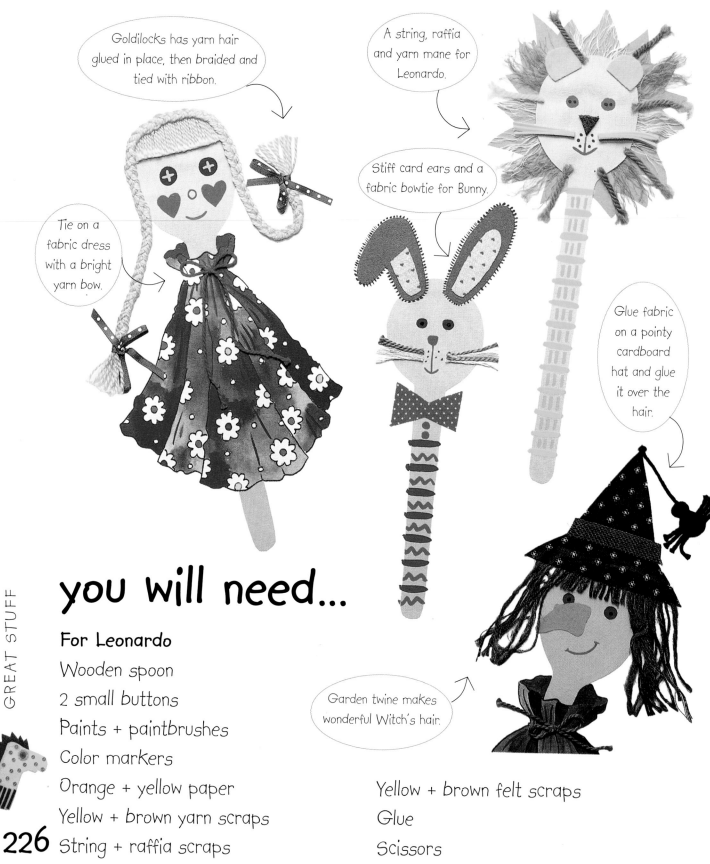

Goldilocks has yarn hair glued in place, then braided and tied with ribbon.

A string, raffia and yarn mane for Leonardo.

Stiff card ears and a fabric bowtie for Bunny.

Tie on a fabric dress with a bright yarn bow.

Glue fabric on a pointy cardboard hat and glue it over the hair.

Garden twine makes wonderful Witch's hair.

you will need...

For Leonardo

Wooden spoon

2 small buttons

Paints + paintbrushes

Color markers

Orange + yellow paper

Yellow + brown yarn scraps

String + raffia scraps

Yellow + brown felt scraps

Glue

Scissors

GREAT STUFF

making a spoon puppet...

Leonardo

 1 Glue button eyes and a brown felt nose in the hollow of the spoon. Draw in a mouth with marker pen.

2 Cut a zigzag mane from orange paper and glue it to the back of the spoon. Cut ears from yellow paper and glue on.

 3 Stick small scraps of yellow and brown yarn, raffia and string to the orange mane.

4 Glue on yellow felt whiskers and paint yellow and orange stripes down the handle.

227

SOCK puppets

you will need...

For Goldilocks

Sock

Yarn, cut into lengths about
   36 cm (14 in)

Yarn, cut into lengths about
   5 cm (2 in)

Ribbon, about 30 cm
   (12 in)

2 small buttons

2 small fabric
   circles or
   round stickers

Sewing thread

Needle

Glue

Give Goldilocks rosy cheeks made of fabric.

Glue on felt ears of different shapes.

Balloons glued on make floppy ears.

Dragon has a zigzag piece of felt glued along the back of his head and neck.

Mouse has a twisted string tail and yarn whiskers sewn in place.

making a sock puppet...

Goldilocks

1 Put your hand in the sock with your fingertips in the toe, and the heel over your knuckles. Push the toe between your thumb and fingers to form a mouth. The heel will be the head of the puppet. Mark where the eyes will go. Take off the sock.

2 Stitch a fringe of short strands of yarn to the head with a needle and thread. Lay the long strands of yarn over the head, overlapping the fringe. Hang an even length down each side. Stitch to the top of the head. Braid the yarn and tie with ribbon.

3 Sew or glue on buttons for the eyes over the markings.

4 Glue a fabric circle on each cheek, or use round stickers.

PUPPETS

MAKE-BELIEVE
masks+headgear

Tea Party Body Masks

Painted Pasta Crowned Masks

Papier Mâché Farm Animal Masks

Googly Eyes Masks

Jungle Masks

TEA PARTY BODY masks

you will need...

For the Teapot

Thick card, about 60 cm (24 in) square (large cardboard box)

Thin card, about 5 x 40 cm (2 x 16 in)

Fabric, 2 strips about 5 x 30 cm (2 x 12 in)

Paints

Paintbrushes

Stapler

Scissors

Glue

Wrapping paper glued onto the card gives exciting results.

Shoulder straps may also be cut from thin card and stapled in place.

Paint a cupcake design for a younger brother or sister to wear.

Wear the lid handle like a hat.

These painted cakes look good enough to eat!

Draw a lid on the teapot with color marker.

making a body mask...

Teapot

1 Cut 2 teapot shapes and one circle out of cardboard. Cut the circle in half for the lid handle.

2 Making sure you have the inner sides together, paint and decorate the outside of the teapot and lid pieces.

3 Staple the 2 fabric shoulder straps to the front and then the back of the teapot. Make sure you leave enough space for your head to fit between the straps.

4 For the lid handle, staple the strip of thin card into a circle to fit round your head. Glue one semicircle to the front of the circle, and one to the back. (The painted side should face outwards.) Stick tape over the staple.

MASKS + HEADGEAR

233

PAINTED PASTA CROWNED masks

Add some shiny stickers and candy wrappers to the crowns to look like fabulous jewels.

Aluminum foil glued to card makes a sparkling crown.

Draw delicate patterns on the foil with a dry ballpoint pen.

you will need...

Thin card, about 25 x 15 cm (10 x 6 in)

Gold card, about 25 x 15 cm (10 x 6 in)

Elastic or ribbon, about 50 cm (20 in)

2 small square stickers

Assorted pasta shapes, uncooked

Gold paint or gold marker pen

Silver paint or silver marker pen

Paintbrushes

Foil candy wrappers

Sequins

Stickers

Hole punch

Scissors

Glue

making a crowned mask...

1   Cut the mask from thin card and the crown from gold card, using the pictures opposite as a guide. Glue together so that the crown overlaps the mask.

2   Cut out eye holes. Stick a sticker on each side of the mask, at the back. Punch a hole in each with the hole punch.

3   Paint the pasta shapes gold and silver (or use marker pens). Glue the pasta in a majestic pattern onto the crown and above the eye holes.

4   Decorate the mask and crown with sequins, foil wrappers and stickers. Add details with gold/silver pens. Knot the elastic through the holes at the sides.

PAPIER MÂCHÉ FARM ANIMAL masks

you will need...

For Buttercup the Cow

Balloon, inflated

Petroleum jelly

Newspaper, torn into strips

Newspaper, rolled up and taped to hold

Egg carton, 2-egg section

Cardboard, about 10 x 25 cm
 (4 x 10 in)

White poster paint
 or emulsion

Brown, red, orange,
 pink, yellow, green
 tissue paper

Raffia or string, scraps

Elastic, about 50 cm
 (20 in)

Scotch tape

Scissors

Glue, diluted with water

Use pink tissue for Buttercup's tender nose and ears.

Buttercup's tail is made from a rolled newspaper.

Glue the buttercup in place where Buttercup's mouth would be.

For Pig's tail, cut a curly shape from card and cover with pink tissue.

Make Pig's nose and ears the same way as Buttercup's, but turn her ears to face downwards!

making a farm animal mask...

Buttercup

1 Cover the balloon with petroleum jelly. Dip strips of newspaper into the glue and paste about 10 layers on half the balloon. Allow to dry. (See page 245).

2 Tape on the cut egg carton nose. Cut 2 ears from card and tape in place. Paste newspaper strips over the joins. Allow to dry.

3 Pop the balloon. Trim the edges of the mask and cut holes for eyes. Paint the mask white all over.

4 Tear up tissue paper, dip in diluted glue and paste layers as before, building up the color. Allow to dry.

5 Glue on a raffia fringe. Make 2 holes on the sides of the mask. Knot elastic through the holes.

6 For the flower, paste tissue on a cardboard flower. Paste tissue on the rolled newspaper tail and tape a bundle of raffia at the end.

237

GOOGLY EYES masks

you will need...

For the Star Mask

Thin colored card, about
    4 × 70 cm (1½ × 28 in)
Thin colored card, about 15 × 10 cm
    (6 × 4 in)
Colored tissue paper, cut into
    thin strips
2 colored chenille stems
    or pipe cleaners
Assorted beads
Star stickers
Color markers
Paper clips
Stapler
Sewing thread
Needle
Scissors
Glue

The decoration of the masks is up to you – make them as colorful as you can!

Make the purple antennae from a single pipe cleaner, folded in half, bent in a Y-shape and threaded with beads.

Use stickers to hold plumes of paper ribbon in place.

These spots have been drawn in with markers, but you could use spot stickers instead.

238

making a googly eyes mask...

Star

 Make a circle with the strip of card to fit round your head. Staple. Decorate with the star stickers.

 Cut 2 paper card circles about 7 cm (2³⁄₄ in) in diameter. Cut holes in the center, to see out of. Draw spirals on the eyes with color markers. Glue onto the headband.

3 Fix 2 small bunches of tissue strips to paper clips. Glue the paper clips onto the sides of the headband.

4 Twist the pipe cleaners together but leave the ends free. Push beads onto the ends. Fold the pipe cleaners in half. Sew or glue the fold to the headband between the eyes.

MASKS + HEADGEAR

239

JUNGLE MASKS

you will need...

For the Tiger

Medium-sized cardboard box

Thin card, about 10 x 20 cm (4 x 8 in)

Raffia, felt or string scraps

Elastic, about 25 cm (10 in)

Paints + paintbrushes

Color marker

Craft knife (be careful!)

Pencil

Parcel tape or Scotch tape

Hole punch

Scissors

Glue

Glue on strips of colored paper for a wild Lion's mane.

Glue soft felt and fabric ears in front of the mane.

Add details to the face and markings with a color marker.

GREAT STUFF

making a jungle mask...

Tiger

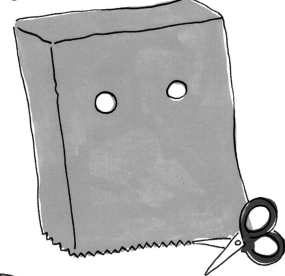

1 Cut the back and bottom off the box using scissors. Cut 2 small eye holes in the front of the box, large enough to see out of. (An adult should help you.)

2 Using the color marker, draw in a nose and mouth, and outline the eyes. Draw the tiger markings in pencil and then paint. For extra comfort, cut out the nose.

3 Cut 2 ears from thin card. Cut 2 slits in the top of the box for ears. Fold each ear 1 cm (1/2 in) from its bottom edge and push through the slits. Tape down the fold on the inside.

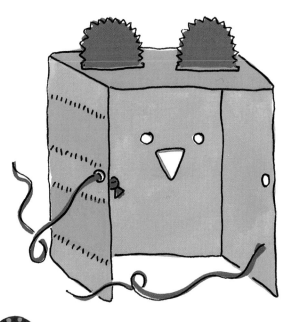

4 Glue on whiskers cut from raffia, felt or string. Unravel some string and glue on wisps to make fluffy ears. Punch a hole on each side of the box. Knot elastic at each side of the mask, so that it fits your head.

241

handy hints

Making a Pattern

Making Papier Mâché

Making a Cone

Drying Orange Slices

Three Simple Stitches

Using Fusible Web

Making a Tassel

Making a Pompom

Making a Stencil

Making Salt Dough

making a pattern

1 Trace the design you want (say, a rabbit) using tracing paper and a soft pencil. Make sure you hold the tracing paper steady while you trace.

2 Lay the tracing paper on card, with the pencil tracing facing down. Transfer the design onto the card by drawing (or gently scribbling) over the back of the design.

3 Cut out the design from the card. This is your card pattern. The pattern faces the opposite way from the original design, but

you can use either side.

4 To use the pattern, draw round it on fabric or paper and cut out the design if you need to. Using a pattern allows you to draw or cut out lots of identical designs.

making papier mâché

1. Tear newspaper into strips. Mix some glue with water, or mix up some wallpaper paste according to the instructions on the packaging.

2. Grease the balloon with petroleum jelly. Paste a strip of newspaper onto the balloon using a paintbrush and the glue or wallpaper paste.

Papier mâché pulp

3. Paste strips of newspaper all over the balloon, building up the layers gradually. Allow to dry for a few days. Pop the balloon. Paint and varnish the papier mâché.

1. For papier mâché pulp, mix newspaper strips or small pieces with dilute glue or wallpaper paste. Knead. Use as a soft clay. Dry for a few days before painting and varnishing.

HANDY HINTS

245

making a cone

drying orange slices

1 Cut a circle from card. The bigger the circle, the taller the cone can be. Cut out a quarter section from the circle, or simply make a cut from the edge to the center.

1 Slice the orange thinly with a sharp knife. An adult should help you with this.

GREAT STUFF

2 Overlap the edges until the circle becomes a cone. The more the edges overlap, the taller the cone will be. Tape or staple or glue the edges to hold them.

2 Put the slices on a baking tray - keep them separate. Bake in a cool oven (100°C or 200°F) until they are dry. (An adult should help you.) Do not burn them.

three simple stitches

Getting Started

Thread the embroidery needle and knot the end of the thread. Starting from the wrong side of the fabric, push the needle through to the right side and begin stitching.

Cross Stitch

Work a row of even diagonal stitches. Then work back along the row, making diagonal stitches that cross the first row.

Running Stitch

Push the needle through to the wrong side of the fabric, then bring it back through to the right side. Continue going in and out of the fabric to make a row of even stitches.

Snowflake/Star/Flower Stitch

Work a group of stitches starting from a central point and stitch outwards. Bring the needle back to the center behind the work and stitch out to make each point of the star.

using fusible web

1 Iron fusible web to the wrong side of the fabric you want to use for your design. An adult should help you.

2 Cut the design you have chosen (say, a star) from the fabric using scissors.

3 Remove the paper backing from the fusible web on the star.

4 Carefully place the star, right side up, on another piece of fabric. Iron over the star to make it stick (an adult should help you).

making a tassel

Paper Tassel

1 Wind yarn, raffia or string 4 times round a rectangle of card. (The wider the card, the longer your tassel.) Cut off the extra yarn.

1 To make a tissue tassel, cut tissue paper into long, narrow strips all about the same width and length.

2 Push a needle threaded with yarn under the yarn at the top of the card. Repeat and pull tight. Make a tight knot, leaving long ends. Cut the yarn along the bottom of the card.

2 Take a bunch of tissue strips and fold it in half. Simply glue the fold in place, or cover and hold with a sticker.

HANDY HINTS

249

making a pompom

1 Draw a large circle and a smaller circle inside it on a piece of folded card, by drawing round 2 different sizes of cup or glass. Cut out the 2 identical rings.

2 With the 2 rings together, wind yarn around the ring. Work slowly round the ring, covering the card completely, and building up the layers of yarn gradually.

3 Keep winding the yarn - the hole in the middle will start to get smaller. You will need to push the yarn through the hole with a yarn needle when the hole is very small.

4 When the hole is blocked, use one blade of a pair of scissors to find the gap between the 2 card rings. With one blade of the scissors still in the gap, cut the yarn all round the ring.

5 Slip a length of yarn between the rings and tie it tightly round the bunch of yarn in the middle. Leave long ends if you want to hang the pompom. Pull the rings off the yarn.

6 Fluff up the pompom and make sure that the tie in the center is hidden. For a multicolored pompom, knot different colors of yarn together and wind onto the rings as in Steps 2 and 3.

making a stencil

1 To make a stencil, first draw your design (say, a fish) on card. Cut out and throw away the fish shape, leaving the fish stencil.

2 The card bridges in a more complicated design (like these stripes) allow you to use different colors in a one-step stencil.

3 Tape the stencil to the surface you want to decorate (in this case, a plant pot), to hold it still. If it shifts, the stencil will not be clear.

4 Pour a little paint in a lid or saucer. Dip a sponge in the paint and dab it onto a paper towel to get rid of excess paint. The sponge should be almost dry. Dab the sponge on the stencil.

5 Slowly build up the color until the stencil shape is finished. Allow the paint to dry *before* carefully lifting off the stencil.

6 For a 2-step stencil, like this butterfly, complete the first stencil (wings) as in Steps 3-5. Carefully tape the next stencil (body) exactly over the first stencil. Complete the second stencil.

251

making salt dough

1 Mix 3 cups of flour, a cup of salt and a drizzle of oil in a bowl. Add about a cup of water to make a soft dough. If it is sticky, add a little flour. If dry, add water.

2 Knead the dough until it comes away from the sides of the bowl. Salt dough will keep for several days if you store it in an airtight plastic bag or box.

3 Roll out the dough or mold it into the shape you need. Sprinkle flour on the work surface to stop the dough sticking. Stick pieces together with a drop of water.

4 Place the dough on a baking tray. Bake a thick piece, like a figure, at 100°C (200°F) for 2-3 hours. Bake a thin piece at 150°C (300°F) for 1½ hours.

5 Tap the back of the cooled piece - a 'thud' means it is not dried, and needs to go back in the oven; a 'ring' means it is dry. Look also for wet dough at the back.

6 When the dough is cold, it is ready to be handled. Paint the dough and add a coat of varnish to seal it.

GREAT STUFF

Patterns

Airplanes
p34

Christmas Stocking
p108

index